Others

Packed with passion, Chick's page-turner grabs the story of Jonah and brings bang up-to-date application to us. Prophetically disturbing and yet warm and accessible – a bit like Chick.

Jeff Lucas, Author, Speaker, Broadcaster

Few people are better placed to challenge us to get out there than Chick. This is not just another book, but an urgent cry that needs to be heard by every believer.

Andy Hawthorne, The Message Trust

The people of God comprise the one community which exists for those who don't belong. Jonah found this out the hard way, but thanks to this great book by Chick Yuill we don't have to get swallowed by a big fish to discover God's adventurous call to others.

Russell Rook, Director, ALOVE, The Salvation Army for a new generation

Chick Yuill is a complex character, a mixture of sharp intellect, artistic passion, forthright communication and often slightly confusing Scottish humour! In this book, he draws on all of these ingredients to provide a provocative call to our founding missionary mandate. It is one of those books that creeps up on you, makes what you think is a good valid point for other readers, the begins to seep into your own soul in the way that o truly prophetic irritants can.

Phil Wall, CEO Sign

Jonah confronts the third millennium! This is ate book written by a passionate man. Read

Rev Stephen Gaukroger, Ser Goldhill

Others

The insistent challenge to a reluctant church

Chick Yuill

Authentic

LONDON • COLORADO SPRINGS • HYDERABAD

13 12 11 10 09 08 07   7 6 5 4 3 2 1

First published 2007 by Authentic Media
9 Holdom Avenue, Bletchley, Milton Keynes, MK1 1QR, UK
1820 Jet Stream Drive, Colorado Springs, CPO 80921, USAOM
Authentic Media, Medchal Road, Jeedimetla Village,
Secunderabad 500 055, A.P., India
www.authenticmedia.co.uk
Authentic Media is a division of Send the Light Ltd., a company
limited by guarantee (registered charity no. 270162)

British Library Cataloguing in Publication Data

A catalogue record for this book is available from the
British Library

ISBN-13: 978-1-85078-757-0
ISBN-10: 1-85078-757-3

Cover Design by Fourninezero design.
Print Management by Adare Carwin
Printed in Great Britain by J.H. Haynes & Co., Sparkford

Contents

Preface

William Booth was a man in desperate need of inspiration. And he needed it quickly. Someone had come up with the bright idea that he should send a telegram around the world, something to stir up the troops and enthuse them for the challenges and trials that lay ahead. The question was, What should he say? The blank sheet of paper lay frustratingly on the desk in front of him; and the eager assistant, whose task it was to deliver the message to the telegraph office, stood impatiently in the doorway behind him.

But Booth was a past master of the *bon mot* – the right word for the right moment. He had used his skill to great effect almost thirty years earlier in 1878 when the proof copy of the Annual Report of the Christian Mission which was under his leadership had been brought to him. His eyes had scanned the copy as he took in the words

> The Christian Mission . . . is a Volunteer Army recruited from amongst the multitudes who are without God and without hope in the world, devoting their leisure time to all sort of laborious efforts for the salvation of others.

The very mention of 'leisure time' was an offence to Booth, who had long before resolved to give every waking hour to the task to which he had been called. And, as for being a volunteer, he'd have none of that. He was a full-time regular or nothing. So, with a little more than a hint of irritation and far more than merely human inspiration, he took his pen, scored through the word 'Volunteer', and above it wrote, very deliberately, **S-a-l-v-a-t-i-o-n**. With that one word he provided the momentum by which a mission agency, largely confined to the East End of London, became The Salvation Army, a world-wide rescue force declaring the good news of the gospel in word and deed.

If one word had done it then, one word would do it now. One word that would be understood in every culture, one word that would remind his soldiers of their commitment to serve and of the constituency that depended on them; and – no small consideration for a man who had learned that every penny had to be raised and spent carefully – one word that would minimise the cost of the telegram. So once again he took up his pen, this time to write a word of only six letters – **o-t-h-e-r-s**. The job was done, the impatient messenger was despatched, and a challenge had been sounded which confronts not only Booth's Army but the whole church to this very day.

Centuries earlier, in a very different setting, a Jewish prophet, Jonah ben Amittai, received a call to deliver a message from God to the people of Nineveh. But Jonah decided that would be taking the idea of serving others much too far. It was one thing to preach to his own nation – the *chosen* people – but to take the word of God *in person* to Nineveh was asking for trouble. It would challenge everything he held dear. And who knows how the Ninevites would react. They might kill him! No, there were others and then there were *others* who were definitely outside of the scope of his theology and his missiology. So Jonah's response was to head in the other direction.

His story is familiar to most of us. So familiar that we have managed to pigeon-hole it as a tale for children. Or we have concentrated all our attention on the big fish that swallowed Jonah and argued about whether we are dealing with literal history or parable, while managing to miss the big message of this brief but profound book of the Bible. But if we read the story with enquiring minds and open hearts, we will surely discover in its mixture of wit and wisdom a God of amazing and extravagant grace who calls his people to reflect his character by living for others whatever their race, class, creed, gender or past.

One

A disturbing call

> The word of the LORD came to Jonah son of Amittai: 'Go to the great city of Nineveh and preach against it, because its wickedness has come up before me.' But Jonah ran away from the LORD and headed for Tarshish...'
>
> *(Jon. 1:1-3a)*

Jonah ben Amittai was not normally afraid of difficult assignments. The reign of King Jeroboam II was hardly an easy time for a man who was called to deliver God's word to his people. Like many of his predecessors, the king sat lightly to the tenets of Israel's historic faith and he was never reluctant to mix a little idolatry with the worship of the true God if it suited his purposes. Jonah must have seethed inwardly as he watched what was happening at court. But despite Jeroboam's unfaithfulness, God remained faithful to his people. Jeroboam might be a very flawed leader, but God had decided that through him he would strengthen Israel's military and political standing and restore her borders, which had been eroded by the repeated attacks of her enemies. And it had been Jonah's task to deliver the promise of God's

favour and to encourage the king in his military endeav-
ours. It was one that the faithful prophet had not shirked
(2 Kgs. 14:23–25).

We might well say that faithfulness was Jonah's middle name. Except it wasn't; it was his family name. *Ben
Amittai* means literally 'son of faithfulness.' Faithfulness
ran in his blood; commitment was part of his make-up.
Here was a man committed to Israel's God, to Israel's
people, to Israel's land. No matter if the king was
unworthy of his office, Jonah would stick to his task.
And what's more, if the name 'Jonah' was anything to
go by, he probably carried it out with a sensitivity that
disarmed even his toughest critics. For his name 'Jonah'
means 'dove', a creature synonymous with gentleness, a
bird with an instinct for heading home at every opportunity.

But now Jonah was confronted with a task of an
entirely different order. Urging the king to secure Israel's
borders was one thing; going up to Nineveh with a message of judgement was quite another. Nineveh was a
long way from home and Nineveh was the chief city of
Assyria, the greatest military and political power of the
day. The problem wasn't simply that it could cost him
his life. Indeed, as the story unfolds we will discover
that death sometimes seemed a desirable option to
Jonah. The real issue was that Jonah was much more
comfortable with his own people than with foreigners,
especially foreigners who seemed to threaten Israel's
very existence. Jonah's faithfulness was bound up with
ensuring Israel's security and protecting her identity.
The whole idea that God was concerned about Nineveh
had simply never entered his head.

Other prophets, like Nahum, had denounced Nineveh
and pronounced God's judgement upon the city in language of shocking violence that painted pictures of piles

of dead bodies and people stumbling over the corpses (Nah. 3:1–7). But he had delivered his message from the safety of Israel and only in the hearing of his own countrymen, who would have applauded his sentiments. Jonah's assignment, however, was a much tougher one. God was asking him to deliver the message *in person* and *in Nineveh* where his hearers might recoil in anger or – even worse in Jonah's thinking – respond in repentance. Of course, he wasn't the first and he wouldn't be the last to have difficulties with his assignment from God. Moses, for example, had protested that he lacked the eloquence of a gifted orator and Jeremiah had argued that he lacked the experience of mature years (Ex. 4:10–13, Jer. 1:4–10). But where others expressed reluctance, Jonah simply refused. They at least had made their excuses; Jonah settled for a quick exit! Nineveh lay to the east and he headed west to Tarshish, a sea-port in Spain. It was just about as far away as it was possible to go in the opposite direction.

Whoever was responsible for setting down Jonah's adventures was a master story-teller. Here we are, just a couple of sentences into the narrative, and already the story has taken a very different direction to that which we might have expected. This is going to be an interesting read. But there's more to it than that. The Book of Jonah is one of twelve short books in the Old Testament which are known as the Minor Prophets. (Their collective title doesn't mean that they are not important, just that they are not as long as the Major Prophets.) But in two very important respects Jonah is different from the other eleven writings that sit alongside it.

Firstly, whereas the others focus on the *message* of the prophet whose name provides the title for the book, all we know of Jonah's prophetic message are eight words in chapter three. The point the writer means us to grasp is surely that the message of the book is in the *story* itself. God wants to speaks to us through the various incidents and accidents that befall the hero – or, more accurately, the anti-hero – of the drama. And secondly, unlike the other prophetic books, there is nothing in the story itself which would allow us to work out the precise historical time when it all happened. (We know that Jonah lived in the time of Jeroboam II only from the reference to him in 2 Kings.) It is as if the writer is saying to us from across the centuries, 'Don't worry about dates. This is a tale for all seasons. The message and moral are just as relevant in your time as when it took place. Don't think of this simply as a historical record of something that happened to one man in a distant age in a far-off country; read it, rather, as the divine revelation of what God is saying to his people in every age and in every culture.'

When you read the story of Jonah in that spirit, it is a fascinating tale, a masterpiece of the short story genre. We may still wonder and discuss exactly what is historical fact and what is parable. We will certainly smile at the vein of good Jewish humour that runs through the narrative. But most of all, we will be challenged by the insistent voice of God, urging us to be and do what the people of God are always called to be and do. And there are already lessons for our time to be reflected and acted upon.

Character alone is not enough

We have remarked on Jonah's gentle, dove-like nature and his faithful commitment to the people of God. Both were admirable qualities, but the entire story demonstrates that they were not enough. In fact, by themselves, they might have been at least partly responsible for the narrowness of vision that kept him from the task to which he was called. The church is right to emphasise personal holiness and morality. It really does matter that I am a faithful husband, that I am honest in my dealings with others, that I give time to my personal devotions, to the reading of Scripture and to prayer. Where we, like Jonah, make the mistake is to imagine that personal piety represents the whole of God's will for humanity and for his creation.

That's why God-fearing, Bible-reading, church-attending Christians have often had nothing to say on matters of civic life and public morality. We have rightly spoken out on abortion and the protection of the unborn child, but wrongly have kept quiet on matters such as the arms trade and the commercial exploitation of the developing world, which have denied a decent standard of living and even life itself to millions of men, women and children. It often comes as a shock to us to realise that God is more concerned about the well-being of millions of people than the minutiae of our personal principles.

Many of us know the story of Eric Liddell from the movie *Chariots of Fire*. He was an athlete, who was willing to give up the chance of a gold medal in the one hundred metres at the 1924 Paris Olympics because of his strict adherence to the principle of Sunday observance. But few of us are aware of the fact that Liddell, having gone to China as a missionary, died a relatively young man just over twenty years later in a Japanese prisoner of war camp, towards the end of World War II. There was some freedom of activity allowed within the confines of the camp and, because of his achievements and reputation, Liddell was given responsibility for overseeing and organising sporting activities. His biographer relates an incident which is seemingly trivial, but actually very significant

> One of the hardest decisions he had to make in the camp was what to do about Sunday games. No, he said, there were to be no games on Sunday; it was a principle from which he had never deviated. But many of the teenagers protested against this and decided to organise a hockey game by themselves despite him – boys against girls. It ended in a free fight, because there was no referee. On the following Sunday, Eric turned out on that field to act as referee. It is a most illuminating detail of his life: he would not run on a Sunday for an Olympic gold medal in the 100 metres and all the glory in the world; but he refereeed a game on a Sunday, he broke his unbreakable principle, just to keep a handful of imprisoned youngsters at peace with each other. It speaks volumes about the man.[1]

Principles were clearly important to Liddell; but people were ultimately more important. Balancing our concern for the first against our care for the latter, especially in a culture where many do not share our standards of personal and sexual morality, will never be easy. But if we are to minister to the needs of a world outside of the church, it is a challenge we cannot avoid. We may rightly feel that the National Lottery is a tax on the poor; but what do we do when its profits are on offer and can be used to support projects and programmes which will benefit those most in need? Promiscuity and drug-addiction among teenagers concern all people of faith and good will and we should do everything we can to encourage young people to live more responsibly; but what do we do when asked to support a needle-exchange or free condom programme to minimise the damage to those who will not follow a better course? Maintaining a good character and following high standards is laudable, but the urge to keep ourselves pure at all costs can easily keep us from serving those in greatest need.

Faithfulness isn't everything

To be recognised for one's faithfulness is commendable. But it too is not without its dangers. Loyalty to a cause, a creed or a culture can easily degenerate into narrowness and sterility. All too often, as with Jonah, our loyalty to the church, to its structures, its programmes and its people have rendered us deaf to God's calling to costly involvement in the world around us. The price of such withdrawal is paid by the wider community that needs us and can be frighteningly high. Sadly, history is replete with examples of the limitations of loyalty.

By 1934 the process of the 'Nazification' of Germany was well under way. In just a few years, every area of life had felt the tightening grip of the stifling hate-filled philosophies of the National Socialist Party. The church had been largely quiet and acquiescent, but a few brave souls had begun to raise their voices as they observed what was happening to various minority groups throughout the country.

But Adolf Hitler, who had been Chancellor of Germany for just over a year at that point, had a simple plan to deal with any unrest from the clergy. He summoned some of the country's leading evangelical pastors to a meeting in Berlin at which he skilfully blended a great deal of affirmation with just a little intimidation to silence the growing criticism. His speech had gone well and he had assured his audience that they had nothing to fear, that their state subsidies and tax exemptions were secure, and that the church was safe under Nazi rule. As the meeting drew to a conclusion he moved among the assembled pastors, shaking hands with this one, offering a complimentary word to another.

The harmonious atmosphere was suddenly disrupted, however, when a pastor from the suburbs of the city, a young man by the name of Martin Niemoller, pushed his way to the front of the group and stood face to face with the Fuhrer. 'Herr Hitler,' he said, 'our concern is not for the church. Jesus Christ will take care of his church. Our concern is for the soul of the nation.' There was an embarrassed silence, and very quickly the other pastors pushed their colleague to the back of the group. Adolf Hitler was astute enough to know exactly what their discomfort meant and a smile crossed his lips as he was heard to say, 'The soul of Germany; you can leave that to me.'

And to their eternal shame, that is just what they did. The cost to the nation and to the world at large in terms of human suffering was tragically high. Millions of Jews, gypsies, disabled people and homosexuals perished in the gas chambers and death camps of the Nazi holocaust and millions of men died in the armed conflict of World War II. The evangelical leaders in Germany were loyal to a church and to a doctrine which made too great a distinction between the sacred and the secular realms. And that very loyalty deafened them to the voice of God and the cries of the afflicted. Faithfulness to received truth and recognised doctrine must always be tested against and authenticated by the willingness to reach out inclusively to all who need God's grace. The New Testament teaches not only that Christ loves the church and gave himself up for her, but also that God loves the world so much that he gave his only Son so that none should perish (Eph. 5:25; Jn. 3:16).

Boundaries can become barriers

It is significant that the only reference to Jonah outside of the little book that carries his name tells how his prophetic word encouraged King Jeroboam II to expand Israel's borders and secure her boundaries. For borders and boundaries are all about defending our security and defining our identity. They describe who we are; they make it clear beyond all doubt who is 'one of us' and who is 'on the outside.' When we bear that in mind, it is not too difficult to begin to understand just why Jonah reacted so vehemently to the call to preach in Nineveh.

If God cares enough about the Ninevites to send a prophet to deliver his message, then boundaries mean very little. The people of Israel may be the 'Chosen People', but, far from bestowing privilege and status on them, what that really means is that God has laid on them the responsibility to share his love and grace with others. National and religious boundaries are, by definition, exclusive; God's message of grace, in contrast, is inclusive.

It is probably true to say that some of the biggest challenges facing the Christian church today focus on issues relating to boundaries and the need to break through them. If we look on the church as the sole or even the primary arena of God's activity, then our default question will continue to be, 'How do we get people to come to church?' We will go on viewing our chief task as inviting men and women to step over the boundary between the church and the world in order to discover God's grace.

The problem with that approach is two-fold. Firstly, it seems clear that the great majority of our peers have no wish to make that leap, for a whole host of reasons. The church appears to them to have little relevance to their everyday lives and concerns. They belong to a culture in which they have become 'jugglers' rather than joiners, a culture of choice in which they may change jobs frequently, select their purchases from a seemingly infinite variety of options, and make lifestyle decisions to suit their needs and desires. In a world of interlocking networks which people move in and out of freely, it makes no sense to them to cross a boundary which will take them into a twilight zone of rules and regulations where choice seems limited and doors are locked.

Secondly, it runs entirely contrary to the nature of the gospel itself. The God of the Bible is not a God who invites people to find him and come to him. Rather, he is the God who comes to us, the God who sends his Son into the world not just to live among us, but to become one of us and to share our humanity. And his Great Commission is not for the church to invite *others to come*, but *for us to go to them*, wherever and whoever they are, with the good news of the gospel. The truth is that we are often as stubborn and stuck as Jonah was and that, if we want to be effective in the twenty-first century, buildings and boundaries will need to be less important to us than active involvement and practical service in our communities.

Boundaries also impact how we allow people to belong. We are beginning to understand that the old paradigm of church membership – in which newcomers to the church first *believed* (gave mental assent to a series of doctrinal propositions), then secondly *behaved* (accepted various rules of conduct, some of which were biblical and some merely cultural), before they were allowed to finally *belong* (became formal members who signed a pledge of allegiance to the local church and/or wider denomination) – needs to be turned on its head. In a post-modern culture, people need to be allowed to

firstly *belong* (be accepted as part of a caring and welcoming fellowship, whatever point they have reached
on their faith journey), in order to secondly *believe*
(explore and discover a living faith for themselves)
which then allows them to finally *behave* (discern and
embrace God's will in every area of their lives). John
Drane has described the kind of church and the kind of
membership called for today

> The need of our culture, however (not to mention the
> gospel imperative itself), is for us to create a community
> where people can feel comfortable to belong, and then to
> be continuously challenging and encouraging one
> another in the belonging and following . . . far from this
> being a mere accommodation of the gospel to the spirit
> of the age, it is actually a more biblical way of being
> church, deeply rooted not only in the teaching of Jesus
> himself, but in the fundamental Christian doctrines of
> creation and incarnation . . .[2]

Intimacy with God and involvement with people are inseparable

In any musical composition that lasts more than a few
minutes, the composer will normally employ a *leading
motif*, a dominant theme that comes at the beginning of
the piece to establish the entire mood and direction of
the music, and which will recur again and again in one
form or another. For the writer of Jonah the *leading motif*
of his story is found in the phrase, 'But Jonah ran away
from the LORD and headed for Tarshish . . .' It not only
highlights the initial action of the central character that
sets up the chain of events that follow; it is the central
theme of the story, which the writer explores from every

angle to take us deep into a truth that lies at the very heart of our relationship with God and the world he has created.

And the truth we are being challenged to face is this: *intimacy with God and involvement with people are inseparable.* Like love and marriage in the old song, you can't have one without the other. And the corollary of this truth is that when you retreat from involvement with people, you inevitably run away from God. If Jonah is unwilling to go to the people of Nineveh, then he is making himself incapable of fellowship with God. In order to avoid the people to whom he is called, he will be forced to flee from the presence of God.

It's obvious that, since God cares about people, we are called to reflect his love and compassion and that any failure to do so disrupts our relationship with him. But there is a much deeper truth here, one that is made plain in Jesus' words on the separation of the sheep and the goats

> Then the King will say to those on his right, 'Come, you who are blessed by my Father; take your inheritance, the kingdom prepared for you since the creation of the world. For I was hungry and you gave me something to eat, I was thirsty and you gave me something to drink, I was a stranger and you invited me in, I needed clothes and you clothed me, I was sick and you looked after me, I was in prison and you came to visit me.'
>
> Then the righteous will answer him, 'Lord, when did we see you hungry and feed you, or thirsty and give you something to drink? When did we see you a stranger and invite you in, or needing clothes and clothe you? When did we see you sick or in prison and go to visit you?'

The King will reply, 'I tell you the truth, whatever you
did for one of the least of these brothers or sisters of
mine, you did for me' (Mt. 25:34–40).

The reason that intimacy with God and involvement
with people are inseparable is that every encounter with
another human being is, in a very real sense, an
encounter with God himself. The ultimate test of our
relationship with God, of our desire to know him and
our willingness to serve him, is found not in the aesthetic quality of our ritual acts of worship or even in
the emotional and spiritual depth of our religious or
mystical experiences. Rather, the ultimate test of our
relationship with God is in how we react to our fellow
human beings who are created in his image, especially
those in need.

This is not to say that we are to be frenetically active,
afraid to be alone, constantly 'doing' for others. That is
the route to emotional breakdown and spiritual burn-
out, not humble service and practical compassion. But it
does mean that authentic worship should always renew
us for effective service, and that in even the most mundane act of service there should be a deep sense of privilege because God is present in the one standing before
us. It will call us to a pattern of work and withdrawal, of
intense involvement with people and refreshing seasons
of prayer such as we observe in the ministry of Jesus
(Mk. 1:29–39).

In her time as Prime Minister of India, Indira Gandhi
must have met many of the most influential people on
the planet. But none made a greater impression on her
than a little Albanian nun who had committed her life to
service in the city of Calcutta. When asked to write a
foreword to a book telling something of the story of
Mother Teresa, she readily agreed. Her words describe

the kind of life that brings God into every human encounter. She refers to the famous prayer of St Francis – *Lord, make me an instrument of Your peace* – and then goes on to say

> It so eloquently epitomises the gentleness, the love and the compassion that radiate from Mother Teresa's tiny person.
>
> Who else in this wide world reaches out to the friend-less and the needy so naturally, so simply, so effectively? Tagore wrote 'there rest Thy feet where live the poorest, and lowliest, and lost.' That is where Mother Teresa is to be found – with no thought of, or slightest discrimina-tion between colour or creed, language or country.
>
> She lives the truth that prayer is devotion, prayer is service. Service is her concern, her religion, her redemp-tion. To meet her is to feel utterly humble, to sense the power of tenderness, the strength of love.[3]

The story of Jonah challenges us all to that kind of living and loving for the sake of others.

Two

Down to Joppa

> But Jonah ran away from the LORD and headed for Tarshish. He went down to Joppa where he found a ship bound for that port. After paying the fare, he went aboard and sailed for Tarshish to flee from the LORD.
>
> (Jon. 1:3)

Odd as it might sound, whenever I read of Jonah's journey to Joppa I think of a five-year-old boy for whom I could still shed tears after more than half a century. It's a simple but poignant story and its relevance will eventually be clear – I promise!

It was 1953 and post-war Britain was gripped with excitement at the prospect of the Coronation of the young Queen Elizabeth II. The new monarch's subjects living in the industrial belt of central Scotland were many miles from the processions and pageantry of London, but they had no intention of allowing the celebrations to pass them by. So it was with real pleasure that the teacher entered the room and shared the good news before she began any lessons for the day: the entire school would be taken to the cinema to celebrate the great event. There was an immediate buzz of excited conversation from the class of five-year-olds who were delighted at the prospect of a whole afternoon of cartoons and other equally innocent entertainment.

But there was one boy sitting towards the back of the class who did not share in the general rejoicing of his class-mates. Not only that, he knew what his duty was and that it was time to make a stand. So very deliberately he left his place and walked towards his somewhat bemused teacher. 'Please, Miss,' he said standing in front of her desk, 'I won't be coming to the cinema. My family are Christians; we're members of The Salvation Army and we don't go to places of worldly entertainment.' Time has mercifully erased from my mind the reaction of the other kids to my stand for truth and righteousness, but I still sometimes wonder what delights they saw and I often wish I could have been there with them that afternoon at the local cinema.

That little incident is imprinted on my mind because it sums up so much of what that generation believed about the relationship between Christian people and the world they lived in. Worldliness was all too easily equated with enjoying any activities outside of the confines of the church and holiness largely meant separating oneself, as far as was humanly possible, from any involvement in the normal pursuits of non-Christian neighbours. The cinema, the theatre, professional sport, dancing and even watching TV on Sundays were all regarded with suspicion.

Of course, it had a simplicity and, it should be said, often a sincerity about it that provided a clear map for negotiating the difficult path of maintaining a purity of life in a world that is full of corruption and temptation. But it failed to do justice to the richness of the gospel.

It took its inspiration from the injunction of the first letter of John: 'Do not love the world' (1 Jn. 2:15). And it took seriously the warning of Paul to the Christians in Rome against being conformed 'to the pattern of this world' (Rom. 12:2). But it tended to forget that those words must be held in tension with the central affirmation of John's gospel that 'God so loved the world that he gave his one and only Son . . .' (Jn. 3:16). When the New Testament writers speak of 'the world' they have a number of related but quite distinct concepts in mind. It is at one and the same time God's creation, whose order and beauty reflects the nature of her Creator; the fallen and sin-scarred arena of life lived outside of God's will; and the world of men and women whom God continues to love passionately and unconditionally and for whose redemption he gave his Son. To understand these complementary truths is to understand that we cannot and must not ever retreat from God's world.

The Epistle to Diognetus was written by an anonymous author, possibly within fifty years of the New Testament period. It is an ancient document but it presents a perfect picture of the way in which Christians need to live in the world

> Christians are not distinguished from the rest of mankind either in locality or in speech or in customs. For they dwell not somewhere in cities of their own, neither do they use some different language, nor practise an extraordinary kind of life . . . But while they dwell in cities of Greeks and Barbarians as the lot of each is cast, and follow the native customs in dress and food and the other arrangements of life, yet the constitution of their own citizenship, which they set forth, is marvellous, and confessedly contradicts expectation. They dwell in

their own countries, but only as sojourners; they bare
their share in all things as citizens, and they endure all
hardships as strangers. Every foreign country is a
fatherland to them and every fatherland is foreign . . .
Their existence is on earth, but their citizenship is in
heaven . . .⁴

The challenge for us is how we apply those timeless
principles and how we overcome the narrow understanding of worldliness which was imposed on the five-
year-old boy with whose story we began this chapter.
And that takes us back to Jonah and his journey to
Joppa. . .

Jonah should have started out immediately and
headed east to Nineveh, a journey of almost five hundred miles. Instead he went south to Joppa, a sea-port
which dated back to the middle of the second century BC
and which is now known as Jaffa, part of the modern
city of Tel Aviv. Assuming that the one hundred miles
from his home-town of Gath-Hepher had to be covered
on foot, it's clear that Jonah was willing to go to some
trouble to reach Joppa. Nor was he put off by the fact
that, at that time, the city was probably under the con-
trol of the Philistines, for so long Israel's arch-enemy.
Joppa might well have been a less than welcoming place
for a Jewish prophet.

For all that, it was not surprising that Jonah should
head for this ancient sea-port, for Joppa was the world-
in-miniature. Its trading links across the Mediterranean
made it a centre of commerce and communication. If
you needed to do business, you needed to come to
Joppa. And, significantly, Joppa figures more than once
in biblical history. Indeed, a brief glance at the references
to Joppa presents in microcosm a model of the inter-
relatedness of God, his people and his world.

The participation of God's people

The building of King Solomon's Temple is one of the high points in the history of Israel. The provision of a permanent house for the Lord, as opposed to the tent employed in the days spent travelling through the wilderness *en route* to the Promised Land, represented a significant moment in Israel's establishment as a nation and as the people of God. 1 Kings and 2 Chronicles in the Old Testament devote thousands of words to precise measurements and descriptions of the materials used and of the great edifice that was erected. Its construction was the supreme religious act of Solomon's reign; and it was to serve as a place of worship, the centre of the nation's life and the focus of her identity as God's chosen people.

But it would not have been possible without Joppa. Solomon wrote a long epistle to King Hiram of Tyre explaining his intention to build the Temple and requesting timber from Lebanon. The reply from King Hiram begins with effusive praise for King Solomon's wisdom in embarking on such a worthy project and ends with the very practical words, 'we will cut all the logs from Lebanon that you need and float them in rafts by the sea down to Joppa. You can then take them up to Jerusalem' (2 Chr. 2:16). And centuries later, when the Temple was rebuilt in the time of Ezra, Joppa was once again the sea-port to which the timbers were shipped (Ezra 3:7).

The simple fact is that it is not only theologically wrong to seek to avoid participation in the world; it is also practically impossible. And yet, again and again throughout the centuries, Christians have fallen into the trap of trying to do just that. Some have opted out of the legitimate political processes open to them; some have dressed in an old-fashioned manner to distinguish themselves from their neighbours; some have sought to create an entire Christian sub-culture within which to do business and follow their leisure pursuits. Such groups not only fail to be salt and light in the world, but they also eventually and inevitably become extinct as their detachment from normal life and everyday reality inevitably stifles their ability to renew themselves and to reach out to their neighbours.

The demonstration of God's power

When we turn to the pages of the New Testament, Joppa becomes even more important for our understanding of our relationship to the world. During Peter's pastoral and missionary journeys, he encountered a group of believers in the city, amongst whom was a woman whose name was Dorcas in Greek and Tabitha in Aramaic – both meaning 'gazelle' in English. Everything we know about her life and character is found in one short and simple sentence: 'In Joppa there was a disciple named Tabitha (which, when translated, is Dorcas) who was always doing good and helping the poor' (Acts 9:36).

But those few words say so much about the role of God's people in God's world. Dorcas was not an apostle; neither, as far as we know, did she possess any of the more spectacular spiritual gifts that would attract attention to her. She was just an 'ordinary' believer. But she was known and loved in the community of Joppa because she demonstrated the power of God in down-to-earth acts of kindness and generosity. When she became sick and died, the room where her body was laid was filled with sobbing widows who had benefited from

Dorcas's dress-making skills (Acts 9:39) and who, in an age long before any kind of welfare state, would otherwise have been poverty-stricken.

The world of the twenty-first century needs to see the power of God demonstrated by God's people in the same practical way. Despite our technological sophistication and our scientific advances, the shameful facts are that thirty thousand children die in the developing world *every day* from preventable diseases, millions still die from hunger or lack of clean water, women and children are sold into sexual slavery, and entire communities lack basic education and health care. The very existence of such injustices is a denial of the love and power of God. Christians need to continue to demonstrate and assert that love and power in acts of personal charity; in lifestyle choices that mean that the affluent West does not continue to use an unfair proportion of the earth's finite natural resources; in supporting economic policies and trading agreements that allow a fair living wage to farmers and growers who supply us with food and clothing; and in political action that persuades governments to direct effort and expertise to humanitarian causes rather than to military hardware and the euphemistically named 'defence industry.'

Dorcas's death coincided with Peter's visit to Lydda which was only twelve miles from Joppa. So her friends and fellow-believers immediately sent for Peter who could not help but be moved by the sight of a room filled with grief-stricken women surrounding her body. Peter had been present on all three occasions recorded in the gospels when Jesus had raised the dead (Mt. 9:25; Lk. 7:11–17; Jn. 11:1–40) so it's not surprising that he did exactly what he had seen Jesus do: he cleared the room and then he prayed. In fact, the parallel is even closer. When Jesus had raised Jairus's daughter he had used the

Aramaic phrase, *'Talitha cumi'* (which means 'Little girl, get up.') Peter's words, using the Aramaic form of Dorcas's name, were, *'Tabitha cumi'*, ('Tabitha, get up') – just one letter different, but with the same result – an undeniable demonstration of God's power in bringing the dead back to life. Little wonder that Luke completes his record of the incident with the statement that 'this became known all over Joppa, and many people believed in the Lord' (Acts 9:42).

The unavoidable implication of the raising of Dorcas is that the power of God, perfectly embodied in Jesus, can still be demonstrated through his people to a needy, watching world. We need a theology that, at one and the same time, is down-to-earth enough to grasp the fact that God's power is shown in practical acts of service, and big enough to believe that the same power can be manifested in seemingly hopeless places, in transforming individuals and situations from death to life. And we need a missiology which will send us into our Joppa – our world and our time – to express that faith in costly and sacrificial obedience to the call to live for others.

The revelation of God's purposes

However, dramatic as the raising of Dorcas undoubtedly was, it was not the climax of Peter's visit to Joppa. Something was about to happen to him that would not only change his life for ever, but that would send the entire church in a new direction. The fact that Peter lodged in the house of a man named Simon, a tanner by profession, while in Joppa (Acts 9:43) is in itself testimony to the fact that God was already beginning to challenge Peter's thinking and expand his horizons. The work of a tanner involved treating the skins of dead animals, a task that would have rendered him ritually unclean in the eyes of conservative Jews like Peter. Obviously, the demands of mission were already beginning to erode Peter's deeply held prejudices. They were now about to be exploded by a revelation from God that would prove to be religious and racial dynamite.

Peter went up onto the flat roof of the house to pray at noon but his devotions were curtailed by hunger and he asked his host for something to eat. While waiting for the meal to be brought to him, he fell into a trance and had a vision of a large sheet coming down from heaven filled with animals, reptiles and birds. A voice instructed him to take the opportunity to kill and eat, an instruction Peter rejected on the grounds that these creatures were ritually unclean and that, consequently, he could never eat them. Back came the reply, 'Do not call anything impure that God has made.' To reinforce the message on Peter's heart and mind, the vision was repeated two more times (Acts 10:9–16). He had not been awake for many minutes before the meaning of the vision became startlingly clear. God's message was about something far more important than just the repeal of some ancient Jewish dietary laws.

Peter's reverie was abruptly interrupted by the arrival of a group of men who had been sent to seek him out by a God-fearing Roman centurion named Cornelius, in response to a vision of his own. Without delay they told Peter that Cornelius wanted him to come to Caesarea and share the gospel. The distance in time and the difference of our culture make it difficult for us to grasp the huge significance of the events that follow. Peter invited the visitors to spend the night at the home of Simon, despite the fact that Jewish custom and practice frowned on such close contact with Gentiles. The next morning he went with them to the home of Cornelius, where his opening remarks made it clear beyond all doubt that his thinking had been turned upside down by the revelation from God

> You are well aware that it is against our law for a Jew to associate with Gentiles or visit them. But God has shown me that I should not call anyone impure or unclean. So when I was sent for, I came without raising any objection. May I ask why you sent for me? (Acts 10:29).

In response Cornelius shared the fact that God had spoken directly to him and Peter confessed his new realisation that 'God does not show favouritism, but accepts men from every nation who fear him and do what is right' (Acts 10:34–35). As Peter went on to share the good news about Jesus, the Holy Spirit fell on Cornelius and his companions, just as he had done on Peter and the other disciples on the Day of Pentecost. The revelation was complete; the gospel is for men and women of every nation and every race! And such a revelation could only have taken place, not in the sacred cloisters of the Temple, but in the everyday world of Joppa and Caesarea.

It was the same for William Booth in the middle of the nineteenth century when he burst in upon his wife Catherine to tell her that he had found his destiny in the mean streets of London's East End. And it was the same for Andy Hawthorne nearly 150 years later in Manchester as the twentieth century drew to a close. God's revelation came through his realisation that the gospel needs to reach the hardest places and the most neglected people

> Manchester (has been described as) 'one of the hardest places to do a mission in the world' . . . As in any major

population centre, there are many social and economic problems that face residents. Crime, unemployment and the breakdown of the family are all instantly recognisable, and housing policies of transferring inner-city communities to out of town estates have only made things worse. . . God has been telling us that we should aim for the toughest places. The result is that we have concentrated on Manchester, a city that's never seen revival, and one that to so many evangelistic organisations is a spiritual wasteland.[5]

Words like that should dispel any doubt in our minds that we must never retreat from our Joppa – our world, our towns, our villages, our cities. For that is where God calls us to be involved, that is where he will demonstrate his power, and that is where he will reveal his purposes.

But that brings us back to Jonah. He's exactly where we've being saying God's people should be. So what's the problem? Why is it all about to go so wrong? The answer is not just that he's taken the wrong route to Joppa. The real problem is that he's there for the wrong reason. . .

The evasion of God's plan

Jonah is in Joppa to avoid doing what God has told him to do. God has a plan that he finds utterly unpalatable and in order to evade the plan, he has to escape God's presence. And, to pick up on the issue with which this chapter began, that's what 'worldliness' really is – using the world as a place of evasion and escape. There's nothing wrong with work, money, everyday responsibilities, possessions, pastimes or entertainment. They're all legitimate aspects of living in the real world. It's only when they become an end in themselves or, even worse, an escape route from hearing and responding to God's voice, that they become dangerous and destructive. We can fall into that trap in two or three ways.

We are all – individuals, churches and denominations – prone to *disobedience*. We know what God wants us to do, but the cost often seems too great and it is easier to take the opposite course. In the end it doesn't much matter whether we run into prevailing culture of materialism or retreat into the sub-culture of our religious ghettoes, the result is the same. We have capitulated to the spirit of worldliness – choosing life outside God's will. David Watson's challenge to Christians rings out as clearly and provocatively today as it did when he first wrote it over a quarter of a century ago

> Christians in the West have largely neglected what it means to be a disciple of Christ. The vast majority of western Christians are church-members, pew-fillers, hymn-singers, sermon-tasters, Bible-readers, even born-again believers or Spirit-filled charismatics, but not true disciples of Jesus. If we were willing to learn the meaning of true discipleship and actually to become disciples, the church in the West would be transformed, and the resultant impact on society would be staggering.'[6]

We can be *sucked into* the prevailing values of our culture so that, without realising it, and still retaining all the trappings of religion, we have lost our purpose in the world. Some years ago Neil Postman, a professor of communication, wrote a book on the obsession of Western culture with superficial entertainment. In a chapter appropriately entitled 'Shuffle off to Bethlehem' he makes a devastating critique of the methods of many tele-evangelists. It is a warning that all Christians and every church must heed

On television, religion, like everything else, is presented, quite simply and without apology, as an entertainment. Everything that makes religion an historic, profound and sacred human activity, is stripped away; there is no ritual, no dogma, no tradition, no theology, and above all, no sense of spiritual transcendence. On these shows, the preacher is tops. God comes out as second banana... What is preached on television is not anything like the Sermon on the Mount. Religious programmes are filled with good cheer. They celebrate affluence. Their feature players become celebrities. Though their messages are trivial, the shows have high ratings, or rather, *because* their messages are trivial, the shows have high ratings. I believe I am not mistaken in saying that Christianity is a demanding and serious religion. When it is delivered as easy and amusing, it is another kind of religion altogether.[7]

We are right to recognise that it is our responsibility to make the gospel relevant. It does not honour God or help those who are not believers when we render the gospel message obscure or inaccessible. But we must beware of the danger of presenting a God made in our image or perverting the gospel so that it becomes just another product to massage the ego and make the life of the prospective consumer even more comfortable.

We can all too easily fall prey to *mistaken doctrine*. The paradox is that such false theology – often based on a few isolated texts – manages, at one and the same time, to separate us from the world and yet render us passively acquiescent to its values. Two obvious examples spring to mind. The evil apartheid regime which held sway for so long in South Africa was shored up and given intellectual credibility by a belief amongst some Christians that the Bible actually supported the theory that some races are inferior to others. When the stern voice of God should have been heard through his people, the church was part of a system which divided men and women on the basis of colour and race.

And towards the end of the eighteenth century when the young William Carey challenged a group of fellow ministers to consider 'whether the command given to the apostles to teach all nations was not obligatory on all succeeding ministers to the end of the world, seeing that the accompanying promise was of equal extent,' he was quickly put in his place by a much older and more educated colleague who told him, 'Sit down, young man! When God chooses to convert the heathen he will do it without your aid or mine!' Thankfully it is a fact of history that Carey's theology and practice far surpassed those of his detractor and he went on to a life of costly and effective missionary service as a co-worker with God.

I don't know of anyone who has expressed with greater clarity the calling of God's people to involvement and service in our world than the late Bishop John A.T. Robinson. His words perfectly summarise all that we've tried to say in this chapter

> The Christian style of life is marked by an extraordinary combination of detachment and concern. The Christian will care less for the world and at the same time care more for it than the man who is not a Christian. He will not lose his heart to it, but he may well lose his life for it . . . The Church's perennial failing is to be so identified with the world that it cannot speak to it and to be so remote from it that, again, it cannot speak to it. These would appear to be opposite and mercifully incompatible sins; but it is remarkable how easy it is for the Christian society and for the Christian individual to commit both of them at once . . . A second mark of the

Christian style of life is an equally paradoxical commitment to . . . 'evangelization' and 'civilization' at the same
time. There has been a perennial tension within the
Christian tradition between saving men's souls and min-
istering to their bodies, between offering them the pure
milk of the Gospel and proffering the cup of cold water
. . . But the dilemma is a false one and comes again from
an unbiblical attitude. For preaching the Gospel in the
categories in which Jesus himself preached it is preaching the gospel of *the Kingdom*, of the sovereign rule of
God over the whole range of human life...There is no
department of the world's life into which (Christians)
arc not commissioned to go. They find themselves concerned with evangelization *and* with civilization,
because in the long run . . . the two are the same – bringing...that divine commonwealth which must ultimately
transform the kingdoms of this world till they become
the kingdom of God and of his Christ.[8]

Three

Stormy weather

Practical atheism

> **After paying the fare, he went aboard and sailed for Tarshish to flee from the LORD.**
>
> **(Jon. 1:2b)**

For the French philosopher, Jean Paul Sartre, atheism was a given. It has often been remarked that the 'loss of God' was not something he ever mourned. But, having disposed of God, he ruthlessly and courageously faced the inevitable consequence of his position. If there is no God, then every man is the author of his own morality and the creator of his own destiny. He spelled out his creed in his famous work *Being and Nothingness*:

> Man can will nothing unless he has first understood that he must count on no-one but himself; that he is alone, abandoned on earth in the midst of his infinite responsibilities, without help, with no other aim than the one he sets himself, with no other destiny than the one he forges for himself on this earth.[9]

The Hebrew prophet, Jonah from Gath-Hepher, was no philosophical atheist. Intellectually he assented to the great truths of Israel's faith. When put to the test, he could readily recite his personal statement of faith: 'I am a Hebrew and I worship the Lord, the God of heaven, who made the sea and the land.' But, to all intents and purposes, he was a *practical* atheist. God might be the centre of his religious creed, but God was not the one who controlled his conduct. Like Sartre, Jonah was counting on no one but himself as he paid his fare and sought to set his own course and forge his own destiny.

Scholars are uncertain as to exactly where Tarshish was. The most likely geographical location is the southern tip of the Iberian Peninsula in what is now southwest Spain. For Jonah the point wasn't so much where it was as where it wasn't! He was aiming to be as far away from God and the people of Nineveh as it was possible to go. He was heading to where God wasn't and where other people – especially those he didn't like – couldn't find him. And he was willing to expend a great deal of energy and a significant amount of money in doing just that.

The truth is that, more often than we would care to acknowledge, churches and individual Christians, for all our ritual and religious observance, take the same route as Jonah. We may be busy, but it's a busyness that takes us in the opposite direction from where God wants us to be. We are often more concerned about maintaining the status quo than extending the Kingdom of God, more anxious about secondary issues of dogma and duty than the primary task of being the means of bringing others into an authentic encounter with the living God.

Bono, the lead singer with U2, is far from being just another rock star with an inflated ego and indulgent celebrity life-style. His passion for social justice and his commitment to raising the issues of Third World poverty with political leaders throughout the world have won him respect from many who would not naturally be drawn to a rock star or his music. But there is still more to Bono. He is a man of deep Christian faith, even if it doesn't always fit into a safe and orthodox framework, and he has an uncanny knack of putting his finger on the blind spots and weaknesses of the church in our generation. Consider this response to a questioner who asked him about his understanding of God

> Well, I think I know what God is. God is love, and as much as I respond in allowing myself to be transformed by that love and acting in that love, that's my religion. Religion can be the enemy of God. It's often what happens when God, like Elvis, has left the building. A list of instructions where once there was conviction; dogma where once people just did it; a congregation led by a man where once they were led by the Holy Spirit. Discipline replacing discipleship . . .[10]

Bono's words remind us that the sin of Jonah is still prevalent amongst us – we can all too easily become men and women of God who carry out the externals of our religion without the presence of God and without the love that will draw others into his presence.

The God of the storm

> **Then the LORD sent a great wind on the sea, and such a violent storm arose that the ship threatened to break up.**
>
> **(Jon. 1:4)**

The failure of God's people across the centuries to truly *be* his people, to live in his presence and to live for others, would make a depressing story were it not for the truth that is about to be revealed to us so dramatically at this point in the tale of Jonah. God is about to act decisively. Despite the prophet's stubborn disobedience, God will not let him go. Jonah is about to experience unforgettably and uncomfortably what is expressed poetically in the magnificent words of Psalm 139

> Where can I go from your Spirit?
> Where can I flee from your presence?
> If I go up to the heavens you are there;
> if I make my bed in the depths, you are there.
> If I rise on the wings of the dawn,
> if I settle on the far side of the sea,
> even there your hand will guide me,
> your right hand will hold me fast (Ps. 139:7–10).

There is no place that Jonah can go where God is not. And there is no way that God will give up on his servant because of his initial refusal. God is a God of persistent grace, continuing to love and forgive and call his people, even when they have rebelled. But this persistent grace is far from being the weak and sentimental permissiveness of an indulgent parent who doesn't mind what his children do just as long as they are happy. God will not give up on Jonah easily, but he will bring him to his senses with a series of events that will bring him to a place where he is both self-aware and God-aware.

We are not wrong when we speak of a God who brings calm to the tempests of life. The story of Jesus stilling the storm (Mt. 8:23–27) has inspired preachers down through the ages and countless people have drawn comfort and strength from it in the face of trials and tragedies. But here we are confronted with an even deeper insight. The storm is the result of 'a great wind' which whipped up the waves and turned the sea into a raging mass of mountainous waves. And there is a deep truth hidden in that little phrase which we too easily miss in translation. Our English word 'wind' translates the word *ruah* which in Hebrew is also the word for 'breath' and 'spirit'; elsewhere in the Bible the same word is used both for the breath of God and the Spirit of God (Gen. 1:2, Ezek. 37:5). What the writer of Jonah wants his readers to realise is that this storm is not just the result of random forces of nature. The Spirit of God is at work in this storm and, however much of a disaster it might appear to the sailors on board ship, he will work out his purposes through it.

God is not only the God of stillness and calm; he is also the God of the storm, and such is his care for his people and his concern to bring them to himself, that he speaks through the storm as often as in the stillness. That is not to suggest that God sends difficulties and disasters to punish us. Quite the opposite. When God allows such things, he does so out of love, not out of anger The profound paradox is that God's love and humility are shown at their deepest when he calls us through pain and suffering. Sometimes that is the one way in which he can get our attention and shake us out of our pride and self-sufficiency; often, like Jonah, we will turn to him only when we know that there is refuge nowhere else. The wonder is that God will accept us even when we come to him only as the last resort. What might seem superficially to be the manifestation of God's anger or indifference is really the ultimate expression of his undying love.

For Jonah the storm is just beginning and he is about to learn some unwelcome and unexpected lessons.

Pagans at prayer

All the sailors were afraid and each cried out to his own god. And they threw the cargo into the sea to lighten the ship.

(Jon. 1:5a)

The prophet who preferred to conduct his ministry within the security of Israel's borders is now out on the high seas, in the middle of a horrendous storm, on board a ship that is threatening to break up at any moment. We might be tempted to think that things could hardly get worse. But that in fact is what happens – at least from Jonah's perspective. And don't ever think that those ancient writers who set down the books of the Old Testament lacked a sense of humour. Jonah's narrow theology prevented him from going to Nineveh with a message of repentance for a city full of Gentiles. Now he finds himself surrounded by an entire crew of pagans at prayer! These men may lack Jonah's understanding of the one true God of Israel, but they are at least reaching out to all that they know of God with all that that they are. And, as the storm rages on, their words and actions will reveal them to be men of some character and integrity.

It is sometimes very difficult for Christians to accept that we have much to learn from good men and women who follow other faiths. Philip Yancey writes of the reactions he received from some quarters and the questions which were raised in his own mind when he wrote a profile of Mahatma Gandhi in *Christianity Today* magazine, to coincide with the release of Richard Attenborough's film on the life of the great Indian leader

Although I have received plenty of venomous letters over the years, I was not prepared for the volume of hate mail the article generated. Readers informed me that Gandhi is now roasting in hell, and that even the devil believes in God and quotes the Bible. 'So it's Gandhi on the cover this month,' wrote one reader. 'Who will it be next month, the Ayatollah?' . . . Another called him 'a heathen agitator who did more than any other person to undermine the influence of Western civilisation' . . . Most of the complaints boiled down to one question: do Christians have anything to learn from someone who rejected our faith? I had concluded yes. Although Gandhi never accepted the claims of Christian theology, he based his life philosophy on principles learned from Jesus. In an odd sort of way, the impact of his life helped convince me of the truth of the Christian faith. I began to see that Jesus unleashed on earth a new kind of power that turned upside down history's basic assumptions . . . When I read the history of Mahatma Gandhi alongside the history of the Christian church, I cannot help wondering what went wrong. Why did it take a Hindu to embrace the principles of reconciliation, humility and vicarious sacrifice so clearly modelled by Jesus himself? Gandhi credited Jesus as his source for these life principles, and worked like a disciplined soldier to put them into practice. What has kept Christians from following Jesus with the same abandon?[11]

Britain is now a multi-cultural, multi-racial, and multi-religious society. It is our duty and our privilege to share the good news of Jesus, the unique Son of God, with men and women of other faiths. But we will be able to do so authentically and effectively only if we first of all have the humility and good grace to treat them with the courtesy and respect they deserve and to recognise what is good and true in their faith and practice. Those who prefer to live within the narrow confines of their own culture, and who are unwilling to make the literal journey to other ethnic communities and the imaginative journey to other religious philosophies, will find it as stormy a time as Jonah did centuries ago.

A sleeping prophet

But Jonah had gone below deck, where he lay down and fell into a deep sleep.

(Jon. 1:5b)

At first glance it might seem a little odd that Jonah should sleep through a storm so fierce that it caused experienced mariners to fear for their lives and to begin to jettison the ship's cargo. But perhaps it's not so odd when we remember that the writer of the story has already told us that Jonah 'ran away' from the Lord. Given Jonah's determination to put as much distance as possible between himself and Nineveh as quickly as possible, and given that these events transpired at a place and time where mass transport was unknown, it is not fanciful to assume that he had covered the hundred miles from Gath-Hepher to Joppa on foot over the course of several days. He must have been completely exhausted – exhausted to the point where he could sleep soundly through a raging tempest.

Some years ago I attended a conference where the speaker was exhorting three hundred or so Christian leaders to work harder. I'll never forget his words, nor the anger they stirred in my heart. 'Christian leaders,' he insisted, 'should always be tired.' It wouldn't have been

so bad if he'd said that Christian leaders should sometimes *get* tired; that would simply indicate that they had
been working hard for some good reason. But leaders
who are always tired make bad decisions and, perhaps
even more to the point, leaders who are always tired are
almost always spending too much of their time doing
the wrong things. They're often more concerned about
the maintenance of the machinery of the church than
about the mission to which the church has been called.
And, more often than we would care to admit, like
Jonah, we're actually running away from what God is
saying to us and wanting us to do. It's all too possible to
fill our lives with frenetic religious activity which really
amounts to nothing more than 'running away to
Tarshish'!

But there's probably more to it in Jonah's case than
mere exhaustion. This is a man in deep denial, doing
everything he can to shut out the world around him. He
should have 'gone up' to Nineveh; instead, he 'went
down' to Joppa; and now he is 'below deck', literally in
the 'innermost part' of the ship. The picture of the
ostrich with its head in the sand springs to mind.
Whatever God is saying to him, and whatever is happening in the world around him, Jonah just doesn't want
to know. And he certainly isn't the last to deliberately
hide away from the storm raging around him.

It sometimes seems to me that Christians have an infinite capacity for denial. I have visited churches whose
buildings were situated in the middle of areas of desperate human need, but who had no real concept that it
was their responsibility to do anything. I have sat with
congregations whose numbers have dwindled over the
decades to the point at which they are facing extinction,
but who take great comfort in the fact that the church
along the road is doing even worse than they are. I have

spoken to mature people whose kids have long ago fled from a church which seems utterly irrelevant to them and to their needs, but who would die rather than change the way they do things. Sadly a spirit of denial still afflicts the church. We can all too easily be locked away while the storm rages around us.

But God is always at work; there is always hope; and there may be more to the sleep of Jonah than is immediately obvious. The phrase 'deep sleep' translates the Hebrew word *tardema*, and it is a word that is often used in the Old Testament for something more than just natural sleep. It is the word that is used for the deep sleep that falls on Adam when God is about to fashion Eve from one of his ribs (Gen. 2:21), when God reveals his covenant to Abraham in a dream (Gen. 15:12) and when David is saved from certain death by the heavy slumber that God sends on Saul's soldiers (1 Sam. 26:12). On one level, Jonah's sleep is the result of exhaustion, a sign of his being in deep denial. But, on another level, God is at work deep within the prophet, bringing rest and renewal as he prepares him for the revelation of new truth.

There are times when we, in our impatience, would dismiss whole sections of the Christian Church as being asleep, even dead and beyond hope or help, but God is not so hasty. He can work his will and bring renewal in what to us are the most unlikely places. Gerald Coates, who had dismissed The Salvation Army as a Victorian anachronism long past its sell-by date, made that discovery at the DAWN Conference in the spring of 1992

> I had spoken to The Salvation Army officers who were there. During the talk the Lord gave me a prophecy which spoke of the breath of God sweeping through them. The Lord would humble them, anointing them with wisdom about when to be in and out of uniform.

Doors would open to them and they would touch even
the royal family, as well as those on the streets.

As I poured out my heart in the prophecy which I felt
the Lord was giving me, my mind was raising questions.
I didn't agree with ranks and uniforms. Would The
Salvation Army hierarchy be prepared to go in a different direction? Then I felt the Lord break in: 'Thank you
for your opinions, but I don't need them.' I felt chastised.
I didn't actually understand what was going on.[12]

Those of us who are committed to this part of the Body
of Christ, and who have gratefully witnessed the partial
fulfilment of that prophecy, long for the day when it will
come to glorious fruition.

Questions, questions, questions

> The captain went to him and said, "How can you
> sleep? Get up and call on your god! Maybe he will
> take notice of us, and we will not perish."
>
> Then the sailors said to each other, "Come, let us
> cast lots to find out who is responsible for this
> calamity." They cast lots and the lot fell on Jonah.
>
> So they asked him, "Tell us, who is responsible for
> making all this trouble for us? What do you do?
> Where do you come from? What is your country?
> From what people are you?"
>
> (Jon. 1:6–8)

Before long Jonah is woken up by a litany of questions
from the captain and the crew who cannot understand
how and why their passenger can be oblivious to the
storm. The first question is the most obvious and basic

one: 'How can you sleep?' and it is followed by the
demand that he, like everyone else on board, should call
on his god. People of all faiths and people of no faith
find it impossible to understand when Christians are
inactive in the face of disaster and injustice. They have
no interest in our theological debates and little patience
with our denominational differences. But they have an
instinctive sense that faith in a loving God should make
us loving people who take the lead in any initiative to
alleviate human suffering and need.

Jim Wallis's book *God's Politics* is an insightful examination of the great issues facing us today and an inspir-
ing call to Christians to translate their faith into political
and community action. He concludes the final chapter
by telling of Lisa Sullivan, a gifted and highly educated
African American woman who committed her life to
action on behalf of the under-privileged and marginalised, but who died at the relatively young age of forty.
When people would lament the lack of outstanding
leadership in the presence of Lisa, she would get angry
and say simply, 'We are the ones we have been waiting
for.'[13] A questioning world will only be persuaded of the
reality of our faith if we grasp hold of the truth of those
words.

The crew, however, have waited too long for Jonah
and his tardiness in prayer leaves them with no alterna-
tive but to look elsewhere for answers. They are facing
the possibility of imminent death and they need to know
who is responsible. The prophet of the God of Israel is
not coming up with any solutions. So they decide to
draw lots – a custom which was widely practised in the
ancient world as a means of discerning what the gods
were saying and which involved drawing sticks or
marked stones from a container. No doubt for those
sailors on the voyage to Tarshish it represented a mixture

of genuine faith and magical practice. To us it seems a strange method of hearing from God, though it was practised even in the earliest days of the church prior to the coming of the Holy Spirit at Pentecost, when they needed to choose someone to replace Judas Iscariot.

But there are lessons to be drawn which are relevant to our own day. God did, in fact, reveal through the drawing of lots that Jonah was the culprit who had brought all of this on their heads. Perhaps we are a little too slow to recognise the willingness of God to act outside the structures and confines of the church when men and women genuinely seek him. In his grace and compassion, he often seems to be less concerned about perfect doctrine and correct church practice than we sometimes are. It seems to be enough for him that there is a desire in the human heart to find him.

Just outside the city of Tucson in Arizona is El Tiradito, or The Wishing Shrine. It is said to be the only shrine in the world to glorify a sinner buried in unhallowed ground. The story behind it goes back to 1880 and centres on a man called Juan Olivera who was involved in a lovers' triangle that resulted in him being shot and killed. Because the ecclesiastical authorities judged him to be a sinner, a church burial was denied to him and he was interred on the spot where he died. People began to make pilgrimages to the place to pray for him and, over time, for the forgiveness of other sinners. Now candles burn there perpetually and flowers and ribbons are placed around the wrought iron stand. Of course, we can dismiss it as just another bit of sentimental Spanish folk religion; and it might be something of an embarrassment to the official Catholic Church; but it stands as a poignant memorial to the fact that men and women will often seek after God in unlikely ways and unlikely places and will, nonetheless, experience something of his grace. The fact that they do so should be a constant reminder to us that they often find their questions unanswered by the church and by their Christian neighbours.

Once the sailors have discovered that Jonah is the one to blame the questions tumble out fast and furious: 'Tell us, who is responsible for making all this trouble for us? What do you do? Where do you come from? What is your country? From what people are you?' And little wonder. They couldn't be anything other than perplexed by a man who would hide below decks, who would sleep through a storm, who would fail to pray to his god, and yet who was ultimately responsible for putting the lives of everyone on board ship in mortal peril. They know next to nothing about their passenger, but they are discerning enough to suspect that he holds the key to understanding why disaster threatens them and what they might do to avert it. Their questions will bring from Jonah a simple creed that indicates the beginning of a realisation in his heart and mind of the enormous implications of what he claims to believe. What that will mean for the prophet and his endangered shipmates will take the story forward to its next dramatic turn.

Four

Creeds and deeds

Doing theology

> (Jonah) answered, 'I am a Hebrew and I worship the
> LORD, the God of heaven, who made the sea and the
> land.
>
> (Jon. 1:9)

The panicking sailors have realised that somehow their
sleepy and reticent passenger knows the reason for the
storm that is threatening their lives. Not surprisingly,
with a series of quick-fire questions, they seek to discover who he is, what he does, where he is from, and to
what people he belongs. On the surface, Jonah's reply is
simple enough. It isn't the whole truth, but it's true as far
as it goes. He tells them his nationality and his religion.
In doing so, he is inevitably 'doing theology', stating his
creed and outlining the essence of his faith, albeit in one
short sentence. Brief though it is, it contains some vital
clues for us as we seek to communicate who we are and
what we believe to a world that often doesn't understand who we really are or what we really believe.

No doubt the very mention of the word 'theology' is enough to have some readers reaching for the nearest bottle of aspirin as their heads begin to ache and they decide that this isn't their kind of book at all! But let's not be too hasty. The simplest definition of the word, deriving as it does from the Greek *theos* meaning *God*, and *logos* meaning *word, teaching or study*, is that theology is the study or teaching about God. And the simplest answer to the question 'Why do we need to do theology?' is that thinking about God is an intrinsic and inescapable part of being human. If you spend any time in the company of children or with a group of men in a pub, you will soon become aware that *everyone* thinks about God. It may be as unsophisticated as the testimony of our neighbour over dinner that 'somebody up there is looking after me.' It may be as confused as the lady on the top of a Glasgow bus who, lamenting to her friend on how bad things were, concluded her musings with the unforgettable sentence, 'If God could only see what was happening to his world, he'd turn in his grave!' It may even be the insistence that God is unknowable or that he doesn't exist at all. But, nonetheless, it is a kind of theology and it is very much part of our humanity.

But there is a more profound and a more relevant answer for Christians to the question 'Why do theology?' We must 'do theology' because theology is the vitally necessary task of reflecting on the faith we hold, exploring our belief system, and prayerfully discerning how those beliefs are integrated into and expressed through our individual commitment as disciples, our corporate life in community as the Body of Christ, and our intelligent and intelligible communication of the faith to a watching world. Without a basic theology we cannot fully live out our faith or share it with those around us. Nor is it enough to be able to recite the creed in church or to be able to repeat the doctrinal statement of our particular denomination. Those are important and provide a standard against which we can test what we believe. But they were formulated in a very different age and expressed in a language which would not be easily understood by our neighbours. We need to be able to share the truth as we have discovered it in a manner that is comprehensible to those around us, and in words and concepts that relate to the concerns of our time and our culture.

Telling our story

The age in which we live is often described as 'post-modernity.' It's a slippery phrase and notoriously difficult to define, but one of its over-riding characteristics is its mistrust of reason and scepticism towards anyone who claims to be in possession of absolute truth. Often Christians have viewed this as entirely negative because it makes it much more difficult for us to make statements like 'The Bible says . . .' and expect people to immediately accept the authority of our words. But that is not the whole picture. This is also the age of story. It is highly significant that, despite the advent of multi-media entertainment and the long-predicted demise of the printed word, the novel remains a powerful force. Equally significant, the cinema is the great teller of stories, stories which are so often woven around the great themes of life and death, fall and redemption, love and relationships. Even the Harry Potter movies are an indication of a longing among adults as much as children for a story with a hint of magic that will take us into a world of wonder and mystery.

Douglas Coupland coined the phrase 'Generation X' to designate the generation born after the 1960s. He describes it as 'the first generation raised without religion.' In one of his novels he tells of three friends who move to the Arizona desert to discover some sort of meaning in life. Two brief excerpts succinctly express what so many feel even if they cannot articulate it

> It's not healthy to live life as a succession of cool, isolated little moments. Either our lives become stories or there's just no way to get through them . . . this is why the three of us left our lives behind and came to the desert – to tell stories and to make our own lives worthwhile tales in the process.
>
> Most of us have only two or three genuinely interesting moments in our lives, the rest is filler . . . at the end of our lives most of us will be lucky if any of those moments connect together to form a story that anyone would find remotely interesting.[14]

In a world where little seems to make sense, people are longing for a story – a big story – that will intersect with their personal stories and bring meaning and direction to their lives. The implication of this fact for us is that the telling of the gospel story must take priority over and provide the foundation for our theology. When we say that we need to 'do theology', we are not implying that we all need to become academics who are able to produce a series of doctrinal propositions which present the old creeds in updated language or that we need to be able to argue (or even understand!) the more complicated aspects of doctrine. Rather, the challenge is for each one of us to reflect upon the gospel story of God's love in Jesus, to explain how it has impacted our personal story and to discern where it intersects with our culture at large and with the lives of our friends and family and neighbours.

In other words, take a lesson from Jonah. In answer to the sailors' questions he tells them about his God *and* about himself: '(Jonah) answered, "I am a Hebrew and I worship the LORD, the God of heaven, who made the sea and the land." He may be, at this moment, a disobedient follower, but he knows that the little story of his life has been touched by the big story of God's plan for the people of Israel; and he knows that the story of his ship-mates struggling for survival in a storm-tossed sea is bound up with the big story of the God 'who made the sea and the land.' For the first time Jonah has brought the different elements of this story together. The crisis is not past, but at last there is hope that together they might discover the meaning of what is happening and some way of escape from the impending tragedy. When imperfect people tell their story of God's plan in their lives, things begin to change!

Holding a conversation

There is something here that is so obvious that we might easily miss it: *Jonah doesn't tell his story until he is forced by the sailors' questions to engage in conversation with them and to answer their questions.* Effective mission and good theology always come out of meaningful conversation and always seek to address the questions of the people around us and the age in which we live. All too often, I suspect, theology is understood simply as paraphrasing the words and summarising the themes of the Bible. Good theology – real theology – however, does even more than that. Of course, it takes Scripture as its primary source and its supreme authority; but it also takes heed of what the church has taught and believed throughout the centuries and brings those great truths into conversation with the needs and concerns of the contemporary culture and the great issues which face us in our generation.

A conversation with our culture will reveal some crucial changes that will impact how we explain our faith and conduct our mission. It will enable us to see that we have moved from *farm to feel-good*. For centuries our fore-fathers lived in an agricultural economy in which life was marked by the rhythm of the seasons and few ever left their native village. Everything changed with the advent of the Industrial Revolution in the eighteenth century. The invention of new machinery made mass production possible and thousands migrated to the cities to find work. That was to hold sway for two hundred years until the decline of heavy industry and the coming of the computer in the mid-twentieth century moved us into what has been described as an information economy. But even that is now being replaced by what might be described as an experience economy.

A visit to the cinema is more than just watching a movie; it is an all-encompassing audio-visual experience with wide-screen images and startlingly realistic surround sound. Eating out is no longer just an opportunity for good food; it's a culinary and sensual experience in a themed restaurant in which the décor, the music, the images, and the dress and role-playing of the staff all contrive to transport you to an exotic world of taste and touch. Digital technology has created a world of virtual reality, of interactive games, in which ever more sophisticated technology will give us ever more convincing experiences.

Such a changing economic and aesthetic culture has brought further changes in its wake. We have moved from *co-workers to consumers*. In an agricultural economy everyone contributed to the toil and shared the produce. With the shift to an industrial economy, that immediate relationship changed. Now you worked in the factory, the shop, or the office, playing only a small part in the manufacture of goods which you might never own for yourself. But the money you earned enabled you to buy the things you needed and wanted for a satisfying life. The co-worker became a worker-customer. The technological advances of the last fifty years have brought the hitherto undreamed of reality of mass-production which, in turn, gives the opportunity for mass-consumption. And that, in turn, has brought us to the latest stage of consumerism – customisation. The message to the consumer today is, 'We'll not only give you a choice – we'll package and adjust it to match it to your needs.' One mobile phone company in Britain had an advertising slogan for some time that described the society in which we live: 'More of what you want, less of what you don't want!'

People who live in a culture of seemingly limitless choice and a world of digital technology begin to think differently. Even your computer is smart enough to check back with you that every decision you make on-line is really what you want to do. ('Are you sure you want to send this document to the recycle bin?) Without even fully realising it, we have moved *from consequences to options*. Popular morality is no longer governed by fear of what might happen if you break the rules. Young women used to be warned that unwanted pregnancy would be the result of promiscuous behaviour. But now our ability to choose our own lifestyle includes our relationships and our sexual behaviour. They are just two more options available to us among many.

At the same time our concern has gone *from ethics to aesthetics*. In the twentieth century Sigmund Freud and psycho-analysis shifted the emphasis from a prevailing external morality that governed our behaviour to an examination of the internal reality of our subconscious drives that lie behind the apparently free choices we make. But our culture has largely given up even on the challenge to discover our true selves by searching within. Now we look to celebrities who can redefine themselves by constantly changing their image. Now our concerns relate to style, appearance, packaging. This is the age of cosmetic dentistry and surgery, of personal trainers and the pursuit of the perfect body and eternal youth, of style gurus and the cult of celebrity, of finding and expressing our worth and identity through the expensive brand names attached to the things we own. More than we would care to admit, we have all been caught up in the journey from ethics to aesthetics!

When we take those changes together, there are themes that immediately become obvious within our culture. The over-riding concerns – some might even say obsessions – of our society centre on experience, personal choice, identity and self-worth. And all are bound up in a deep desire to belong, a search for true community. It is with these issues and the people who feel them deeply that we must hold our conversation, rather than some of the things that have exercised us in the past. Like Jonah, we need to answer the questions with which we are confronted rather than the ones we'd like to be asked.

There is a little point in doctrinal debates about the precise nature of the inspiration of Scripture, for example. No-one is arguing about questions of absolute authority. The inspiration of the Bible, its God-breathed quality, will become obvious only as we tell the story effectively. And though the gospel has much to say about sin and forgiveness, it is not the whole of the good news nor is it always what troubles people today. Their immediate concerns centre on self-worth, a search for identity and a longing for community, and the gospel has much to say about those things. Good theology helps us start where people are, allowing the story of Jesus to speak to their ultimate need for an authentic, life-transforming experience.

Building a community

There is one glaring weakness in Jonah's creedal statement to the pagan sailors. He is a man on the run from God and from the people to whom God has called him, and consequently he is attempting to share his faith while he is separated from his people and his community. What we believe cannot in the end be communicated just in words. The story can only be properly told and the conversation can only be properly held by the community of God's people living and working in the larger community around them, expressing by their deeds the truths they declare by their words. It is interesting that Jonah introduces himself by saying 'I am a Hebrew . . .' 'Hebrew' is a word that would often have been used by foreigners with reference to Jews. But this is the only time in the Old Testament that the phrase is used in this way by a Jew to describe himself. We might have expected him to say, 'I am an Israelite . . .' but that would have emphasised the fact that he belonged to the people with whom God had made his covenant; and he was running away not only from the people of Nineveh, but from God and the people of Israel. Or he might have described himself in the words, 'I am a prophet . . .', but that is precisely what he wasn't at this moment. When Jonah describes himself as a Hebrew he is, in effect, admitting that he is a man who has deserted his community and his calling.

The sailors were longing for someone who knew the true God and who could bring his power to their fragile craft. On our fragile planet where, despite the veneer of our affluence we are becoming increasingly conscious of impending disaster, there are many who are searching for a creed that is more than words, more than a statement of doctrinal propositions and theological cleverness. They are looking for a place – no matter whether it is a majestic cathedral or a company meeting in the front room of a house in the street where they live – where the mundane and the menial are touched by the miraculous, where people matter and where they are allowed to explore faith, even if such an exploration creates a messiness and a fuzziness so that it is difficult at times to judge who really 'belongs' and who is just looking. They are looking for a place where there is the possibility of an encounter with God in which the mystery of the divine and the meaning of life intersect. They are looking for a place where the frailty of humanity and the authenticity of following Jesus stand side by side. In short, they are looking for a place where faith can be learned and lived and where theology can be grasped both by the intellect and the imagination and can be lived out by ordinary people in the everyday world. It is our responsibility to create such a place where 'others' can be accepted as being part of 'us.'

Good deeds and wise words

> This terrified them and they asked, "What have you
> done?" (They knew he was running away from the
> LORD, because he had already told them so.)
>   The sea was getting rougher and rougher. So they
> asked him, "What should we do to you to make the
> sea calm down for us?"
>   "Pick me up and throw me into the sea," he
> replied, "and it will become calm. I know that it is my
> fault that this great storm has come upon you."
>   Instead, the men did their best to row back to land.
> But they could not, for the sea grew even wilder than
> before. Then they cried to the LORD, "O LORD, please do
> not let us die for taking this man's life. Do not hold us
> accountable for killing an innocent man, for you, O
> LORD, have done as you pleased."   (Jon. 1:10–14)

The first part of Jonah's story is about to reach its climax,
but the focus of the story-teller is more on the sailors than
on their passenger. And no wonder. For the conduct and
conversation of these pagan seamen is such that they put
the prophet of the true and living God to shame. *He* had
refused to listen to God; *they*, recognising something of
the power of God in the storm, are more than willing to
seek counsel from Jonah whom they recognise as a
prophet. *He* was totally lacking in any compassion for the
thousands who might perish in Nineveh; *they* are so concerned about the life of just one man – Jonah – that,
despite the increasingly rough sea and the danger to their
own lives, they attempt to row back to land. *He* had
turned his back on his responsibility to declare God's
word: *they* take full responsibility for the terrible choice
they face and plead with God for forgiveness.

In every town and city in our land there are men and women of goodwill and principle who are not Christians. Some of them would make no claim to faith; others are devout followers of other religions. They often put us to shame by their hard work and high standards and they are often deeply committed to serving their communities. If we are to take seriously Jesus' call, not only to preach the truths of the gospel but to live out those truths as we become salt and light to a dark world, we must be willing to recognise the worth of such good people and to work alongside them. Of course, we must take every opportunity to share the gospel with them, but we will do so graciously and humbly, recognising that we have much to learn from them.

But perhaps the most telling thing about these men is seen in their question to Jonah when they grasp the significance of the fact that he is hiding from the God he claims to worship: 'What have you done?' It is the very same question that God asks of Adam and Eve when they try to hide from him in the garden after their disobedience in eating the fruit of the tree that he had forbidden to them. It is a dramatic moment and the significance of it should not be lost on us: for Jonah's narrow religious and nationalistic prejudices are being confronted not just by the fact that the sailors behave so much better than he has done. Here is something he was not prepared for. *Not only does God love these pagan sailors, he is speaking through them!*

Many of us still find it difficult to grasp that God can speak through men and women who are outside of his church. Indeed, his word can often come to us through those who are critical of us. Some years ago Tony Campolo wrote a book with the splendid title, *We have met the enemy and they are partly right* in which he looked at the writings of great figures such as Karl Marx, Sigmund Freud and Friedrich Wilhelm Nietzsche. We need to heed Campolo's words

Too often those of us who rant and rage from our pulpits against the materialism of Karl Marx, the sexual preoccupations of Sigmund Freud, and the God-is-dead philosophy of Friedrich Nietzsche know almost nothing about these declared enemies of religion . . . A religious group matures and improves only by correcting its flaws and usually the enemies of that group can help it to see those flaws better than its friends can . . . There is far more to be learned from them than from friends who flatter and patronise us, but fail to tell us the truth that hurts. I hope that by studying the arguments of our enemies we will recognise our sins, confess them, and work to cleanse ourselves of them.[15]

All truth is God's truth, whatever quarter it comes from and God can speak through those who make no profession of faith. There are many men and women of wisdom and goodwill outside of the formal boundaries of the church. We need to be willing to listen to them, humble enough to learn from them, gracious enough to dialogue with them, and sufficiently grounded in God's word that we can discern what is right and good from what is mistaken and unhelpful in their philosophies.

Man overboard

"Pick me up and throw me into the sea," he replied, "and it will become calm. I know that it is my fault that this great storm has come upon you." . . .

Then they took Jonah and threw him overboard, and the raging sea grew calm. At this the men greatly feared the LORD, and they offered a sacrifice to the LORD and made vows to him.

(Jon. 1:12,15,16)

Something is beginning to stir in Jonah's heart. If he lacked the compassion and imagination to envisage the suffering of the people of Nineveh, the plight of the sailors is so immediate and obvious that he cannot ignore it. For the first time since we have met him, he takes responsibility for what has happened. Not only that, he is willing to die for the sake of his travelling companions. Of course, some commentators have been astute enough to notice that incidents later in the story reveal that Jonah may have had something of a 'death wish' and that, consequently, his motives may have been mixed. But that's oddly comforting in a way. As sinful human beings, our motives are rarely if ever completely pure. The most selfless things we do are often tinged with more than a little self-interest. But God uses us just the same. So, as Jonah is thrown overboard, the storm immediately subsides and calm prevails.

But God is not finished with Jonah. His story has only just begun and there is still much more for him to learn. Indeed, even by the end of his story as we have it, God's work in him is far from complete. The same could be said of the sailors who are left on board ship as Jonah goes over the side to an apparently watery grave. Their fear of the storm is replaced by a different kind of fear – a sense of awe in the presence of the living God who, in Jonah's words, 'made the sea and the land.' They even offer sacrifices and make vows to God. But there is no suggestion that they renounce their pagan gods or become devout followers of the God of Israel. It is a telling reminder to us that God does not give up on any of us, that he is willing to do his work slowly in us, and that conversion is as much of a process as a crisis.

And those are the things that we will constantly need to keep in mind if we are serious about living and working for others.

Five

Great events

A great fish

> **But the LORD provided a great fish to swallow Jonah, and Jonah was inside the fish three days and nights.**
> **(Jon. 1:17)**

My wife is an avid listener to the radio, particularly Radio 4. Whenever she's doing anything around the house, she'll usually have a radio somewhere near her. She says that she prefers it to the TV because you don't have to watch, so you can listen and do a dozen other things at the same time. She's right, of course, but there is just one flaw in her argument. When you're doing a dozen other things you don't always listen as closely as you might. And that's why she ended up so confused by a recent broadcast. For the life of her, she couldn't understand why an entire programme had been devoted to three academics discussing the merits of Blu-Tack. It's a useful substance for sticking things on walls without damaging the paintwork, but claims that it has had a major influence on western civilisation seemed to her to be somewhat over the top. So she stopped what she was doing to listen just a little more closely. It was only then she realised the subject under discussion was not *Blu-Tack*; it was *Plutarch*, the great Greek biographer and essayist! It really does make all the difference when you pay proper attention.

Everybody knows – or thinks they know – the story of Jonah and the whale. The man and the sea mammal go together like fish and chips. But again it's a case of not paying enough attention. For a start, there's no mention of a whale in the biblical record, just a 'great fish.' And there are just three brief references to the fish in the entire tale. It's certainly part of the story, but it's not the whole story. Unfortunately, this focus on 'the whale' has done two things. Firstly, it's meant that most people have no idea what the story of Jonah is really about; they don't know what follows on in the narrative and they've failed to grasp the message and meaning that we are meant to grasp. And secondly, it's meant that for too many sincere people, the main issue of the book is whether this is 'really true' or not. Indeed, for some very sincere Christians, believing that the fish really did swallow Jonah has become one of the key tests of a genuine respect for the authority of the Scriptures! Ironically, a part of the Bible that is all about breaking through barriers to reach out to others has become a dividing line that separates people of different opinions.

So let's clear this up before we get on with what this part of the story is all about. Deciding whether Jonah is a literal historical record or a vivid parable is not a deal-breaker in deciding who is a true believer and who isn't. Equally sincere Christians with equally high regard for the Bible, including some of the greatest minds in church history, have held different opinions on this for centuries. For example, Origen who lived in the second and third centuries AD, knowing that the Bible incorporates different kinds of literature such as poetry and parable, believed the story was allegorical; but Augustine of Hippo a couple of hundred years later was convinced that it was literally and historically true.

What we all need to bear in mind is this. History is never completely objective; it is always written from a particular point of view. (The stories of Scotland's battles with her powerful neighbour to the south were taught to me at school from an angle that shocked my English cousins!) In the same way, the Bible writers were not primarily concerned about bland or detailed historical records for their own sake. They always wrote from the perspective of faith in a loving God who was fully involved in the lives of his people, and they were less concerned about the 'mechanics' of an event than about its meaning and message. If we were able to ask the writer of Jonah, 'Is this "real" history from which you've highlighted the moral for us, or is it a kind of parable based on the experience of God's people?' the question probably wouldn't make sense to him. What is 'real', he would probably respond, is what this tells us about God and his attitude to people.

But someone always asks, 'What do *you* think?' so I'll tell you. We learn so much almost every day about strange events that are not easily explained, that I don't find it all that difficult to believe that a great sea creature could swallow a man and that he might survive. And, even more to the point, since my faith commits me to believe in the *big* miracle of a God who raised Jesus from the dead, I can cope with the fact that he could send the right fish at the right time to save Jonah from drowning. Whatever position you take, you'd do well to heed the advice of the preacher I heard say, 'The fish didn't let Jonah stick in his throat; so don't you let the fish stick in yours!' Now let's get to the really *big* stuff . . .

A great God

The real focus of attention is not a great fish but a great God. Jonah had no trouble in repeating his creed to the sailors when he told them that he worshipped 'the LORD, the God of heaven, who made the sea and the land.' He could recite it with his lips and he even believed it in his head, but it certainly hadn't touched his heart. In reality his god was too small: a god who was confined to the borders of Israel and cared only for the chosen people, and he could be escaped simply by running away to sea.

Such a puny concept, such a travesty of the true and living God, may seem ridiculous to our more sophisticated minds. But Jonah's narrow-minded and mean-spirited religion has survived across the centuries and infected the Christian church more often than we would care to admit. In Henry Fielding's novel, *Tom Jones*, we encounter it in the tragi-comic figure of Parson Thwackum who gives expression to it in his unforgettable declaration of his faith: 'When I mention religion, I mean the Christian religion, and not only the Christian religion, but the Protestant religion, and not only the Protestant religion, but the Church of England.'

Sadly there are those in every part of the church, not only in long-established, traditional denominations but also in newer church streams, who imagine that God is confined to their statement of doctrine, their way of worship and their approach to mission and evangelism. They existed in the early day Salvation Army and the wise and saintly Samuel Logan Brengle had a winsome but effective way of dealing with them. Brengle had given up academic respectability to join the Army; he loved everything it stood for and he was as committed to it as any man could be, but he had no doubt that God was bigger than any one part of his church. His biographer explains

how he would respond to those who thought God wore
a uniform and resided in a Citadel

> (Brengle is) no subscriber to the vindictive principle:
> 'Orthodoxy is my doxy; heterodoxy is your doxy.' If he
> comes across a comrade in The Salvation Army who has
> adopted the attitude that 'The Army is the only way to
> heaven . . .' he will reply: 'Well, brother, that magnifies
> the Army all right. But it does seem to minify God,
> doesn't it.'[16]

The big fish that swallowed Jonah didn't simply happen
to be passing that way by some lucky chance – or
unlucky from Jonah's point of view! It was 'provided'
(the Hebrew word could equally well be translated 'des-
ignated' or 'appointed') by God in the same way that,
earlier in the story, the wind that raised the storm at sea
was 'sent' by God; and, later in the narrative, the vine
and the worm are also the result of God's initiative. The
point we – and Jonah – are meant to grasp is this: God is
not just the God of one people or one nation; he is not
confined to one region or one sphere of human activity;
he is, indeed, a great God, the God of creation and the
God of history.

And for the first readers of Jonah's story the arrival of
the big fish would have had a significance that is not
immediately obvious to us. They would have known
from the mythology of their Canaanite neighbours of the
great sea monster Leviathan, a creature of such brutal
strength and force that it featured in tales of primeval
conflict, wrestling with the gods and threatening to
bring chaos. The assumed existence of such a fearsome
beast meant that the sea itself was understood to be a
dark and dangerous place where even the gods of the
nations feared to pass. In telling of the 'great fish' that is

appointed by God, the narrator of Jonah is doing more than just recording a historical incident; he is inviting his readers to see that Yahweh, the God of Israel, unlike the gods of the surrounding nations, is truly Ruler of all creation and Lord of all created things, however powerful or dangerous. The universe is not just some cosmic accident; it is not even the result of primeval forces; it is the work of the Creator who sustains it by his word of power. And history is not just a series of meaningless random events; God is active within it and everything that happens ultimately serves his purposes.

That's not to suggest that there is always an easily discernible pattern to the events of life or that things don't ever go wrong. The old King James translation of the well-known verse in Romans chapter eight was both inaccurate and misleading: 'And we know that *all things work together for good* to them that love God, to them who are called according to his purpose' (Rom. 8:28: AV, my italics).

The New International version renders it more accurately and much more helpfully: 'And we know that *in all things God works for the good of those who love him*, who have been called according to his purpose' (NIV, my italics). The hard truth is that 'things' don't always work out well. People get sick and suffer, young people sometimes die, accidents happen, relationships go wrong – and all these things happen to people of faith as much as to anyone else. But the greater truth is that, somehow, God works in and through all things, pleasant and unpleasant, for our ultimate good. A great God is Lord of every circumstance, every accident, every tragedy. And people who have discovered that truth can begin to live radically and dangerously for the sake of others, knowing that nothing can ultimately separate them from God's good purposes.

But here is an even deeper wonder in the greatness of God. The Creator God who reigns over all and who can summon the elements and the creatures of the deep at his command is, at the same time, the God who allows human freedom and choice. There is an inescapable touch of humour and irony here: the great sea monster obeys God's command without a murmur of dissent; the winds blow, the sea rages, the vine grows, and the worm gnaws as and where God commands; but Jonah – *the dove of faithfulness* – resists him and runs. The God of the universe will follow us to the ends of the earth, he will find us wherever we hide, he will face us with the truth of his limitless love, he will even harness the forces of nature to arrest our attention, but he will never force us to do his will. That is a great God!

A great hymn of praise

From inside the fish Jonah prayed to the LORD his
   God. He said:
"In my distress I called to the LORD,
and he answered me.
From the depths of the grave I called for help,
and you listened to my cry.
You hurled me into the deep,
into the very heart of the seas,
and the currents swirled about me;
all your waves and breakers
swept over me.
I said, 'I have been banished
from your sight;
yet I will look again
toward your holy temple.'

The engulfing waters threatened me,
the deep surrounded me;
seaweed was wrapped around my head.
To the roots of the mountains I sank down;
the earth beneath barred me in forever.
But you brought my life up from the pit,
O LORD my God.
When my life was ebbing away,
I remembered you, LORD,
and my prayer rose to you,
to your holy temple."

(Jon. 2:1–7)

I've sung hymns in some very unusual places. Singing 'How great thou art' standing at the very southern tip of India where three seas meet and helping to make up an impromptu choir perched on a ledge in Fingal's Cave on the Island of Staffa spring to mind as the most memorable. But those were the kind of settings where the wonder of nature lifted the spirits, and the glory of creation made it difficult *not* to burst into songs of praise. Singing a lengthy psalm all on your own from deep inside a fish is a very different matter! I guess it must have been partly from sheer relief. The belly of a fish may not be five star accommodation, but it's infinitely preferable to death by drowning.

Most of Jonah's prayer-song draws on concepts and phrases found in the Jewish Psalter, but the words must have taken on a whole new and deeply personal significance for the beleaguered prophet. His prayer as he plunged into the sea had been answered, albeit in an unexpected manner. He was still breathing and he could not but be grateful. A gracious God had come to his rescue, even though the runaway prophet remembered him

only 'when (his) life was ebbing away.' It is a truth we
have encountered before in the story and one we will
meet again before it is over. God is exceedingly patient
with his reluctant servants. There is hope even for the
most unwilling disciples and for the most undeserving
churches.

And we cannot help but notice that it is not until he
reaches the point of death that Jonah begins to come to
his senses. When he says at the beginning of his song
that he called for help 'from the depths of the grave' the
literal translation of the Hebrew is 'from the belly of
Sheol' which was the place of the dead. In Jewish thinking at that time, it was a dark and desperate place of
shadowy non-existence from which there was no escape
and no hope of ever living in the light of God's love
again. It's as if he's been to hell and back. But that's
where Jonah has discovered God and begun his journey
back to life. Until this point in the story, all his movements have been downwards – down to Joppa, down to
the lower decks of the ship, down to the icy deeps of the
sea, down to the very 'roots of the mountains.' But now
there's an upwards motion as his prayer rises to God's
temple.

There is a powerful parallel with our day and our situation as the people of God in the twenty-first century.
Across the western world many mainline denominations are reaching a place of crisis. Their membership is
declining rapidly and their influence is decreasing expo-
nentially. Of course, there are bright spots here and there
from which we take comfort and try to derive hope and
encouragement. But these are the exception and we
ignore the larger truth at our peril. Most of these denominations have tweaked their internal structures and
sought to adopt a variety of methods of evangelism or
models of church but often to little avail. Now it is time

to be ruthlessly honest on this matter for the sake of the Kingdom of God. It is no longer a question as to whether these denominations will die in the twenty-first century. Unless the culture around us reverts to that of the 1950s – something that, to say the least, seems highly unlikely – death is certain.

The question, however, is: what kind of death will it be? If we try to hold on to our outmoded structures and our narrow and limited thinking, it will surely be the death of extinction. But if there is a willingness to acknowledge the truth, to meet with God at the place of death, to follow Jonah and, 'with a song of thanksgiving' to sacrifice everything, to be willing to die for the sake of others, it might well be the kind of death that leads to glorious resurrection. It will not be painless; we will not come out of it unscathed; and much of the church may well be unrecognisable from how it looks today; but we will, in fact, have touched the very heart of the gospel which Jonah could only dimly realise but which the followers of Jesus should know only too well. It is in dying we live, and that is as true for congregations and denominations as it is for individuals. Eddie Gibbs puts it bluntly but powerfully and even encouragingly

> God hasn't given up on denominations, for, in the over-
> all scheme of things, it is the denominational churches
> that make up by far the greatest segment of world
> Christianity. It is hard to imagine that they are all des-
> tined for the scrap-heap. While it is often said that it is
> easier to have babies than raise the dead, it might just be
> that God has the greater miracle in mind. This is not to
> suggest that denominations can emerge intact. Far from
> it! For the present cultural upheaval from modernity to
> post-modernity (however the latter term is defined) will

necessitate not merely the structural re-engineering of
denominations but their death and resurrection . . . It is
those churches that refuse to bury their nostalgia and
dismantle their defences that will fail to survive.[17]

It is a death that will take us all the way from a maintenance mentality to a mind-set of mission-before-every-
thing-else; from a concern about formal membership to a
commitment to call men and women to radical and
authentic discipleship; from an emphasis on denominational policies and practices to an energising pragmatism
that is willing to try whatever works in communicating
the whole gospel to the whole person in the whole community; from a strategy of invitation, which tries to figure out how we can get people to 'come to church', to a
missiology of incarnation which is willing to take the
church and the Lord of the church to people wherever
they are; and it will call not just for pastors who are content to preserve denominational traditions and preside
over the 'rites of passage' for the faithful few, but for pio-
neers who will manage change and birth a vibrant new
church out of the ashes of the old. Make no mistake, it
will be far scarier than jumping over the side of a ship
and far more exhilarating than plunging into the icy
waters of a raging sea!

And, just in case any of us is tempted to imagine that
such costly dying to self is something only for denominations, churches and large ministries, let's repeat that
the challenge to take up the cross and attend our own
funeral is a call to every individual too. We will all need
to come in some way or other to the point of death to our
personal preferences, our narrow prejudices, and our
selfish ambitions if we are to fulfil the gospel imperative
to live for others and bring them into the joy and liberty
of the Kingdom of God.

A great escape

> "Those who cling to worthless idols
> forfeit the grace that could be theirs.
> But I, with a song of thanksgiving,
> will sacrifice to you.
> What I have vowed I will make good.
> Salvation comes from the LORD."
> And the LORD commanded the fish, and it vomited
> Jonah onto dry land.
>
> (Jon. 2:8–10)

Jonah's psalm of praise comes to a conclusion with a recognition that clinging to worthless idols results in the forfeiture of God's grace, a state which he contrasts with his own new-found determination to fulfil his vows in a spirit of sacrifice. Clearly we have reached a turning point in his experience, a place of repentance and commitment. Ironically, however, it has taken a near-death experience to bring the prophet of Israel to the same place as the pagan sailors reached immediately after his unceremonious departure over the side of the ship. Sadly, it remains a fact of experience that it often takes more to move the resistant people of God than those who are outside the structures of church and organised religion. Any church leader who has sought to encourage change in a congregation will witness to the fact that when prejudice and stubbornness are allied with a narrow view of God's grace and purpose, things are mighty difficult to shift!

But there does come from Jonah's lips a final declaration of profound truth: 'Salvation comes from the LORD.' His plight remains desperate. The belly of a fish is no place for a permanent residence. But at least he is acknowledging that his hope for deliverance comes not from his nationality or his race but from the God of heaven who made the sea and the land. The question that remains to be answered in the remainder of the story is simply this: 'Will Jonah hold to this truth if God calls him again to declare his message to the people of Nineveh?'

It is one thing to raise our hands in worship and to make bold and emotional declarations of faith in God's grace when we are deeply moved and when we sense the presence and favour of God. It is quite another thing to stand by them when we face the hostility or apathy of those with whom we feel we have little in common. But that's where the real test of our faith lies. God *is* concerned for me and my family and my church; but he is at least as concerned for the asylum seekers, the teenagers with ASBOs, the drug addicts and the homeless who live nearby. And the test of how deeply I have appreciated and appropriated his grace will be seen in how readily and generously I share it with them by responding to their spiritual and practical needs.

So when, at God's command, the fish vomits Jonah onto dry land, it is a great escape. Yet again there is a robust irony about the story. For Jonah is about to discover that his deliverance from the deep means that there is, in fact, *no escape* from the task to which God has called him. Nineveh is still there and the task remains to be done...

Six

Second time around

Life can be very unforgiving in some things. Consider the case of Mr Fydekker, a Fellow of the Royal Society no less, who wrote to the Letters section of *The Times* back in the days when it was something of a coup in England to be able to lay claim to having heard the first cuckoo heralding the imminent arrival of spring. Even at this distance in time and, despite the somewhat more formal language employed in those days, you can sense the pride and confidence of the letter-writer

> From Mr Fydekker, FRS, February 6, 1913:
> 'Sir,
> While gardening this afternoon I heard a faint note which led me to say almost immediately to my under-gardener, who was working with me, 'Was that the cuck-oo?' Almost immediately afterwards we both heard the full double note of a cuckoo . . . There is not the slightest doubt that the song was that of a cuckoo . . .'

However, less than a week later, *The Times* published a second letter from the same person. This time, however, the tone was much less confident and far more contrite

From Mr. Fydekker, FRS, February 12, 1913
'Sir,
I regret to say that I have been completely deceived. . .
The note was uttered by a bricklayer's labourer in the
neighbourhood of the spot whence the note appeared to
come. I have interviewed the man, who tells me that he
is able to draw cuckoos from considerable distances by
the exactness of his imitation of their notes. . .'[18]

I confess that I have not researched the archives of *The
Times* for the years that immediately followed 1913, but
I strongly suspect that Mr Fydekker wrote no more letters, at least on the subject of cuckoos as the harbingers
of spring. A man who has misheard the call once is not
likely to be in a hurry to make the same mistake again.

A different man

> Then the word of the LORD came to Jonah a second
> time: 'Go to the great city of Nineveh and proclaim to
> it the message I give you.'
>   Jonah obeyed the word of the LORD and went to
> Nineveh.
>
> (Jon. 3:1–3a)

Jonah's experience was very different from that of Mr
Fydekker. For a start, Jonah had not misheard the call; it
was unmistakable and, as we have seen, he was willing
to go to great lengths to try to shut it out of his heart and
mind. And if anyone had cause to be embarrassed, it
was Jonah. By any reasonable standards of justice, he
definitely did not deserve a second chance. Not only had
his disobedience left the people of Nineveh bereft of

God's message, it had also put the lives of innocent sailors at risk. Surely God would leave him to regret his wilfulness, to reflect on what might have been and to repent of his hard-heartedness.

Instead, what actually happens is that, no sooner has the fish vomited Jonah on dry land, than God is back with the same call as before: 'Go to the great city of Nineveh and proclaim to it the message I give you.' Again one of the dominant themes of the story sounds loud and clear – we might mess up on the task in hand, but God never gives up on us. And, second time around, it seems as if Jonah has learned his lesson. He obeys the call and heads for Nineveh, though I suspect that he went a little like the old sailor at the conclusion of Samuel Taylor Coleridge's famous poem, *The Rime of the Ancient Mariner*

> He went like one that hath been stunned,
> And is of sense forlorn:
> A sadder and a wiser man,
> He rose the morrow morn.[19]

Jonah had learned painfully and a great cost just how human disobedience impacts others. Nothing would ever erase from his memory the fear on the faces of his shipmates as the storm raged or the fact that, had they died, their blood would have been on his hands. Of course, the very fact that God continues to call and use him is in itself assurance of forgiveness, but even for-giveness doesn't wipe out all the consequences of a wrong action. We mentioned in chapter One the failure of large sections of the church in Germany in the 1930s to speak out against the atrocities of Nazi rule. That God forgave his cowardly church is not in doubt; that the consequences of their sin remain as a terrible stain on the pages of history and as a blot on the conscience of Christian people for all time is equally beyond dispute. We are all sadder and (hopefully) wiser men and women because of their failure.

However, it is not simply our failures that change us. We often assert glibly that an experience of God makes us happier people. That is certainly true, but it is not the whole truth. There is also something about an encounter with the living God that forces us to confront the reality of pain and suffering. And it is rare for any of us to escape the battle with doubt as we reach into the deep mysteries of faith.

Dennis Potter, arguably the finest television dramatist Britain has ever produced, was certainly not an orthodox Christian. The almost unbroken success of his writing was in sharp contrast to his personal and life-long battle with illness, a debilitating combination of psoriasis and crippling arthritis. His comments on his struggles to discover God for himself are full of profound insight. In a Radio 4 interview in 1976 he described the process beginning to take place in his life

> (I believe in) a loving Creation (which) is in continual battle with, and tension with, and obvious opposition to, the misery, cruelty, crudity and pain of an imperfect world . . . I have changed, but even within what people I suppose would call faith I have maintained doubt . . . Whatever faith I have, or hope to have, it would be . . . walled in by doubt. And doubt is the necessary response of man at this period of time to such awesome claims by religion. But yes, I've changed . . . I cannot now live without . . . some idea of a loving God.[20]

Eighteen years later in the summer of 1994 and just a few days before he died from cancer, Potter gave a last

interview on BBC television. In a deeply moving conversation with Melvyn Bragg, he expressed his conviction that religious faith is not an easy cure-all for the ills
of life, but rather a longing for God which is in itself a
deep hurt, but one that brings meaning to life

> Religion to me has always been the wound, not the
> bandage . . . I don't see the point of not acknowledging
> the pain and the misery and the grief of the world. And
> if you say, 'Ah, but God understands . . .' that's not how
> I see God. I see God in us, or with us . . . in some shred
> or particles or rumours; some knowledge that we have,
> some feeling why we sing and dance and act; why we
> paint, why we love, why we make art.

Followers of Jesus, of all people, should recognise the
wound of which Potter speaks. It is bloody and gaping
and stands at the very heart of our faith in the figure of
a young man impaled on a cross, suffering and dying for
a sin-sick world. It is a wound that will never be healed.
The Risen Lord still bears the scars of the nails; the heart
of God still breaks for a wounded world. To be true to
our Lord, we must never give way to easy sentimental-
ism or glib triumphalism. We live with the problem of
pain, the sickness of a lost world, and the consequences
of our own spiritual and moral failures. There is no
magic bandage, no escape from the cost of following a
suffering Saviour.

But Potter is also on the right track when he points to
those 'rumours and feelings' that cause us to love and
sing and make art. They are just as much the insistent
call of God as the word of the Lord that came to Jonah.
They are cause for celebration because they draw us
back to the One from whom we so often and so easily
run away. And, to an extent that neither Potter in our

day nor Jonah in his ever fully appreciated, God really is with us and in us, not simply in those 'rumours' but in the reality of the Risen, living Jesus. It's not a bandage to patch up all the hurts and take all the pain away. We are called to share the searing wound that always opens when divinity and humanity meet; the wound that is both the inescapable burden and the indescribable glory of true, obedient discipleship. We are all, at best, wounded healers, bringing the brokenness and failures of the years to the service of others at the behest of our Lord.

Yitzhak Perlman was born in Tel Aviv in 1945. Tragically, at only four years of age, he was struck with polio, causing permanent paralysis in both his legs and leaving him reliant on crutches and leg-braces for the rest of his life. Despite his handicap, the boy began to demonstrate an extraordinary talent as a violinist and today he is one of the world's leading classical musicians. On an unforgettable evening, he came on to the stage and made his usual preparations, laying down his crutches, adjusting his leg braces, placing the violin under his chin. But as he began to play, one of the strings broke. The audience fully expected that the violinist would leave the stage and that the concert would be delayed while he made the necessary running repairs to his instrument. But, carried by the momentum of the music, Perlman was in no mood to stop. He continued to play, adjusting the remaining strings, changing the strokes of the bow, and all the time playing with breathtaking technique and artistry. The audience was spellbound and, as the last note faded, they stood to their feet and expressed their appreciation in thunderous applause. Perlman's response said as much about his willingness to overcome physical handicap as it did about his ability as a musician. 'It is my task,' he said, 'to make music with what remains.'

Jonah has been disobedient; he has neglected his calling; he has caused hurt to others; he has almost drowned; he has been to the belly of Sheol; he has been vomited out by a huge fish; he is definitely damaged and flawed. But God still calls him and it is gloriously possible for him to 'make music with what remains.' Thank God that no less can be said of us and of the church: our lives and our history contain many a discordant note, but we can still sing the Lord's song to a world that is longing for the divine music.

A different God

Reading the story of Jonah is, for me, a little like looking at a painting of a glorious landscape on a clear spring day. Picture the scene: in the foreground there is a great plain, a vision of pastoral beauty where the gently waving grass and the vibrant green foliage delight the senses; but, in the background, towering over everything, stands a majestic and rugged mountain whose slopes rise through the snow-line to the distant summit which is shrouded in mist and cloud. And, for all the pleasing beauty of the rustic lowlands, it is the mountain that draws the eye and the imagination of the observer. What timeless mysteries might wait to be discovered on the mountainous heights?

Jonah is the central character in our story, a sad misfit of a man who, for all his failings, fascinates us by his humanity and the honesty of his portrait presented to us by the writer. But standing over everything, greater than anything else on the landscape of the narrative, is the character of God, drawing us to himself, inviting us to ponder the mysteries and unexplored wonders of his infinite love and grace. And, if we respond, what we will discover will be a very different God to the one that has been presented to us by much of our formal, academic theology for centuries. To appreciate that difference, and its importance for a church that is called to live and die for others, we need to give some thought to the early church fathers, to the world in which they lived, to some of the challenges they faced, and to their efforts to make the gospel relevant and accessible to their culture.

Early western Christianity faced two particular challenges. One was the pagan mindset of many of the earliest converts whose thinking and religious practices were steeped in polytheism, the belief that there were many gods; Christianity, cradled as it is in Judaism, is a monotheistic faith and the church was looking for all the help it could find in establishing that central truth in the thinking of its converts. The other challenge it faced was to develop an apologetic, a sturdy and intellectually robust defence of the faith that would demonstrate that the God of the Bible was the universal God and that the Christian gospel was compatible with the accepted and respected academic learning of the day. They found the help they were looking for in contemporary Greek thinking.

The foundations for their work had been laid by Philo, a great Jewish thinker who lived from 25 BC–45 AD and who sought to reconcile biblical truths with Greek philosophy. His thinking and theology drew heavily on concepts derived from Plato. Plato had taught that, because God is perfect, it is, therefore, logically impossible that he can change, since any change would mean that his perfection would be destroyed. Similarly, Plato's God is beyond emotions such as joy or sorrow; to experience these would inevitably disturb the perfection of his soul. A God like this is essentially beyond love; in Plato's view, one can only love what one lacks and God, as a totally self-sufficient being, lacks nothing outside of himself. The only relationship such a deity can have with the world is that of 'the unmoved mover' as Aristotle was to describe him, a God whose divine power has brought the universe into being but who then stands utterly transcendent above it, untouched by its struggles and woes.

Picking up on this way of thinking, Philo speaks of a God who dwells in eternity, beyond all time, who is unknowable, absolutely transcendent and ineffable – utterly beyond human reason and understanding; a God who is omnipotent, omniscient, omni-present, totally self-sufficient, unchanging, and immune to any passions. Building on these foundations, the church fathers developed their theology of the nature of God, a theology which has held sway for centuries and which, to a considerable extent, governs the thinking of many Christians to this day. The problem is that, while this approach served the early church well in the struggle with polytheism and in its need to integrate theology with the learning of the day, it seriously compromised and constrained the God we encounter not only in the story of Jonah but throughout the entire Bible.

Whereas classical theology concentrates on what we might call the 'substance' of God's being – his 'one-ness' and his self-sufficiency – the Bible writers have little or no interest in that kind of abstract metaphysical speculation. Instead, they emphasise God's capacity and desire for relationship. Not only is God *capable* of relationships with us, his very nature is love. All his other attributes – his omnipotence and omniscience and omni-presence – are bound up in and, indeed, are subservient to the fact that he is defined by love. Consequently, the God who encounters Jonah is not a distant God untouched by emotion. Quite the opposite. He is a God who cares passionately for Israel and Nineveh, a God who persists in seeking a relationship with his creatures even when they, like Jonah, turn their back on him, a God who is always willing to give his people another chance.

When we come to the New Testament, the fact that God is a God of relationships is written large on every page. The earliest disciples were, of course, devout Jews and the central pillar of their faith was the conviction that God is not many, but One. It is, therefore, all the more remarkable that their experience of a God who has revealed himself as a loving Father throughout Israel's history, who has come amongst us in the person of Jesus Christ, and who lives within the individual Christian and in the community of believers, led early Christian thinkers to reflect and conclude that the only adequate understanding of that experience is found in the conclusion that the One God is also Three – Father, Son and Holy Spirit. From all eternity God has been in relationship – that is his very nature as revealed in the church's experience – and there is no other way to speak of God than to push language to its very limits and talk of the Trinity in the Godhead.

But that very recognition leads us to an understanding that is in conflict with much of the effect of the legacy of Greek philosophy on our theology. We cannot in all conscience continue to embrace a theology that insists that a God whose very being is dynamic relationship is, nonetheless, untouched by emotion and deep passion. Those two things are mutually exclusive. If we – and our theological mentors – had read our Bibles more attentively, with eyes unclouded by the veil of Greek philosophy, we would see on every page evidence of God's love for humankind, his disappointment over our failures, his longing for our willing obedience, his anger over injustice and his concern for the poor and oppressed.

Nor can we persist in teaching – as so many doctrinal manuals still do – that God's omniscience and fore-knowledge mean that he never ultimately changes his mind, or that his perfect will can never be thwarted in any way. Love, by definition, awaits the reaction of the 'other', the one who is loved; love, by definition, can be rejected and spurned; love, by definition, may need to take a different tack to reach the hardened heart of the reluctant and resistant beloved; love, by definition, is always vulnerable, always at the mercy of rejection, never able to predict or predetermine the free choice of the object of its deep affection. And it makes no sense to argue that divine love can over-ride those self-imposed limitations; if it does, then it may be divine but it is no longer love. We are attributing to God not omniscience, but the ability to do what is logically impossible.

If the argument above seems lengthy and passionate, it is not primarily because of a concern for sound doctrine, important as that is. Nor is it simply because it lies at the heart of the message of the story of Jonah, though it does. Jonah thwarts God's plan by his nationalistic and narrow-minded attitude to the people of Nineveh and God has to come up with plan B. And, as we shall see as the story unfolds further, God will gladly change his intention of bringing punishment when the city repents. It will not do to dismiss such passages as 'unsophisticated theology' to be demythologised and reinterpreted by our more subtle understanding. To do so is to compromise the integrity of Scripture on almost every page. Yes, we can be sure that love will triumph in the end; that is the nature of love, to persist until the biggest barrier is breached and the hard-est heart is broken. But there will be many a twist and turn in the upward path before that day is reached.

We argue the case with such vehemence because we have for too long painted a picture of a God who knows everything in advance, who in certain theologies even wills some to salvation and some to damnation for reasons that we cannot fathom, and who is about as attractive to sensitive, sincere, seeking people as a medieval despot or a malevolent dictator. How can we bow before a helpless baby born of a teenage unmarried mother, follow a carpenter turned wandering, penniless, homeless rabbi, and declare allegiance to a crucified Saviour on the one hand and then, on the other hand, articulate a theology which presents God as an all-powerful, all-knowing Being who often appears to do nothing in the face of sickness and suffering? It is little wonder that those who have witnessed some of life's most terrible tragedies shake their heads and prefer to embrace a chilling but honest atheism. It is time to tell them of a vulnerable God who, in giving humanity freedom of choice, willingly limits his power and who, in humility and compassion, seeks a relationship with us that will enable us together to face the evils of the world and transform it, not by coercion but by costly and committed caring. In short, it is time to tell them of a God whose power is constrained by love, whose knowledge is limited by the freedom he gives us to choose, and whose very being is love for others.

A different sign

It is at this point that we can begin to understand the remarkable place accorded to Jonah in the teaching of Jesus. In response to a demand from the Pharisees and teachers of the law for a miraculous sign, Jesus took his cynical interrogators back to the story of the prophet from Gath-Hepher

(Jesus) answered, "A wicked and adulterous generation asks for a miraculous sign! But none will be given it except the sign of the prophet Jonah. For as Jonah was three days and three nights in the belly of a huge fish, so the Son of Man will be three days and three nights in the heart of the earth. The men of Nineveh will stand up at the judgment with this generation and condemn it; for they repented at the preaching of Jonah, and now one greater than Jonah is here (Mt. 12:39–41).

Two aspects of Jonah's story are highlighted in Jesus' answer: his time in the belly of the fish (which is viewed as a 'type' of the resurrection, prefiguring the death and raising of Jesus), and the impact of his message in bringing the Ninevites to repentance, which Jesus contrasts with the hard-heartedness of the Jewish leaders of his day.

Considering all the faithful characters to be found in the pages of the Old Testament, it is ironic that Jesus turns to Jonah as a sign of God at work. But, if we reflect on all that we have said in this chapter, it is, perhaps, not all that surprising. A loving and patient God manifests his power and brings to fruition his plans in the lives of unlikely and even uncooperative people. More than that, he has so designed us that, when we *are* truly ourselves, living out his purposes in self-giving love, then we are most like his Son; and when he looks on us he sees nothing less than Christ in us. That is ultimately the purpose of our lives on earth.

No one ever captured that truth more powerfully than the great Jesuit poet, Gerard Manley Hopkins. In one of his finest sonnets, he writes of what he calls 'inscape', the capacity of each created thing to assert its own nature and express its unique individuality. In so doing, each thing declares the glory of God who created it.

And, when that glory is expressed by human beings in lives that are obedient to God, the life of Christ is made actual again in us. The language is dense and rich and does not yield to cold logic in the manner of everyday prose. But, if you will quietly ponder these ten brief lines, especially the last three, allowing their profound meaning to wash over your heart and mind, you will understand more fully the wonder of the fact that to 'be ourselves' is nothing less than to be open to and to express the indwelling grace of the Son of God

> Each mortal thing does one thing and the same:
> Deals out that being indoors each one dwells:
> Selves – goes itself: myself it speaks and spells,
> Crying *What I do is me: for that I came.*
>
> I say more: the just man justices;
> Keeps grace: that keeps all his goings graces;
> Acts in God's eye what in God's eye he is –
> Christ – for Christ plays in ten thousand places,
> Lovely in limbs and lovely in eyes not his
> To the Father through the features of men's faces.[21]

Seven

Walking to Nineveh

Large cities

I have lived most of my adult life in large cities and I
love them. I enjoy the occasional retreat to the quietness
of the countryside and I can appreciate and be
impressed by the majesty of the mountains, but there's a
buzz about a city that is unmatched by anything else,
something that draws you in and captivates you with its
own peculiar beauty. Even that great poet of the English
Lake District, William Wordsworth, could not escape the
attraction. To his great surprise, he fell under its spell
when crossing Westminster Bridge in London one morning in the summer of 1802. If you've ever looked over a
city from a suitable vantage point, you'll understand
something of his wonder

> Earth has not anything to show more fair:
> Dull would he be of soul who could pass by
> A sight so touching in its majesty;
> This City now doth, like a garment, wear
> The beauty of the morning; silent, bare,
> Ships, towers, domes, theatres and temples lie

> Open unto the fields and to the sky;
> All bright and glittering in the smokeless air . . .[22]

It seems that millions of my fellow human share my sense of being irresistibly drawn to cities, as the following newspaper article from January 2007 makes clear

> Some time this year or next, humanity will officially cross the line from being a rural to an urban species. For the first time in history, more of us will live in cities and urban areas than in the countryside, and the social and environmental implications of this transition to a predominantly urbanised world are enormous.
>
> UN figures for urbanisation, published this week in the State of the World 2007 report, show that more than 60 million people – roughly the population of the UK – are added to the planet's cities and suburbs each year . . .[23]

To put that figure of sixty million into even sharper focus, what it means is this: *today there are 180,000 more people living in cities than yesterday and tomorrow there will be 180,000 more*; and that will go on day after day for the foreseeable future. It is not difficult to understand why this trend of urbanisation has developed such momentum. Cities are viewed – and to a considerable extent are – places of opportunity. They act like a magnet to those looking for jobs, education, and a better place to raise their families. The escalation in the number of megacities is an inevitable outcome of economic growth in the world's largest economies in countries like China, Brazil, India, Japan and the United States of America. It also reflects the fact that the economic value of industry and services has far outstripped that of agriculture, forestry and fishing to the extent that around two-thirds of the world's workforce is now employed in industry and services.

At their best, cities are good places in which to live. To quote again from the newspaper article above: 'In general, the more urbanised a nation, the higher the average life expectancy and the literacy rate and the stronger the democracy . . .'[24] In addition, cities provide a concentration of amenities and activities that would be impossible in a more rural context. My own city of Manchester provides a typically impressive list of facilities and opportunities: it is in a phase of ongoing development and construction with new office blocks and houses going up all over the city; there are several universities with a student population of around seventy thousand; it is a major centre for both broadcasting and printed media; there is an enormous variety of opportunities for entertainment including cinemas, theatres, concert halls and professional sports venues; and there are museums, parks, and other sites of cultural and historic interest.

But city life is much more complex and definitely not as uniformly positive as the picture we have painted above would suggest. Despite the fact that millions of people are now better off than their parents and grandparents and that they live in larger communities than at any previous time in human history, there is considerable evidence to suggest that we have become less connected and more isolated from each other. The busyness of life, the improvements in housing and the ready availability of entertainment at the flick of a switch make us less eager to participate in activities outside the confines of work and home.

We have become 'jugglers' rather than 'joiners.' For example, membership of the local gym, unlike belonging to more traditional clubs, does not demand either the commitment to attend regularly or the responsibility to relate to other members. Consequently, there has been a loss of what is sometimes called 'social capital', a useful collective term to describe the meaningful relationships between people in any society, relationships which manifest themselves not only in family units and friendships, but in commitment to such activities as church membership, involvement in voluntary groups like Rotary or Parent-Teachers associations, and playing a part in civic duties such as voting or standing for the local council. The results of this decline can be seen in increased loneliness, depression and emotional illnesses, as well as a loss of cohesion in society.

These, however, are predominantly the issues facing the more affluent city dwellers. It might well be argued that they pale into insignificance when set alongside the problems of the poor in our cities. One of the characteristics of urban life in the twenty-first century is that deprivation and extreme poverty often exist cheek by jowl with almost obscene levels of wealth. Again, David Satterthwaite's article succinctly homes in on the terrible truth of much city life today. He may be writing primarily about the situation in developing countries, but all that he highlights can be seen in the big cities of the western world

> Around a billion urban dwellers – a sixth of the planet's population – are homeless or live in crowded tenements, boarding houses or squatter settlements, often three or more to a room. Most have to live with inadequate provision for water, sanitation, healthcare and schooling. Many are denied the vote, even in democracies, because they lack the legal address required for voter registration. They are often exploited by landlords, politicians, police and criminals. The global extent of urban poverty is underestimated because it is usually measured by poverty lines

based on the cost of food, ignoring the high costs that most low income urban dwellers have to pay for renting a room or bed and for water, healthcare and transport.[25]

Large cities, with all their opportunities and all their difficulties, are an increasingly significant aspect of life in the twenty-first century. And, such is the nature of western culture in the developed world, even those of us who make our homes in smaller towns and villages cannot completely escape the challenges of city life. To a greater or lesser extent, the issues of the large city, including crime, homelessness, and societal breakdown ultimately impact us all wherever we live. The questions we face as the people of God are these: how should we relate to our cities and how can we reach them with the good news of the gospel? For the answers to those questions we must now turn back to Jonah as he accepts his commission to declare the word of God to Nineveh.

Long journeys

> Jonah obeyed the word of the LORD and went to Nineveh. Now Nineveh was a very important city – a visit required three days.
>
> **(Jon. 3:3)**

If they were asked what they knew about Jonah, most people would probably respond that it's the story about a man who was swallowed by a big, scary fish. Actually, it's much more about a man who was called to a big, frightening city. The original listeners to this tale would have been far less troubled by the reference to the sea creature than by the mention of Nineveh. The origins of the city date back to the sixth millennium BC and, by the time of Jonah, it was one of the principal cities of the powerful Assyrian Empire whose armies were feared for their ruthlessness in battle and their history of subduing weaker nations in military conquest. Little wonder that he was at first reluctant to accept the assignment to preach in Nineveh.

But now, following his unceremonious return to life and land, and in response to God's repeat of his command, Jonah is on his way to the great Assyrian city. As the story unfolds, the dramatic turn-around has taken just a couple of sentences and it all seems so sudden. It certainly must have been startling to the prophet. His home town of Gath-Hepher was probably little more than a fair-sized village where he would know just about everyone and they would know him. Now he's standing in the middle of a city of 120,000 souls, a city that takes three days to walk across on foot. At least it would be a less claustrophobic prospect than three days in the belly of a fish.

However, his apparently sudden appearance in Nineveh hides a series of related truths that would have been much more obvious to his contemporaries and to the immediately succeeding generations who heard the tale. Going to Nineveh, far from being a quick day-trip, actually meant a journey of around nine hundred miles across desert routes. Not only that: the verb used here is different from those used in the opening sentences back in chapter One where we were told that he 'ran away' from the Lord and 'went down' to Joppa. Although our English translation says simply that he 'went' to Nineveh, the Hebrew word 'halak' means literally that he *walked* – all nine hundred miles! If it was hard work to escape from God, it took an even greater effort to reach Nineveh. A journey of that length would have taken months and would have given him opportunity for many hours of reflection. It would also have meant that Jonah, the prophet for whom boundaries had become barriers, was now forced to cross one boundary after another – not simply the literal territorial and geographical borders of cities and nations, but the equally real boundaries of culture and religion that had previously separated him from the people to whom God had called him.

But this is all part of Jonah's continuing education for life and mission. For the verb 'halak' provides more than just a description of his physical progress on foot; it also emphasises the fact that he goes at God's command and in God's company. In both the Old and New Testaments 'walking' is frequently used as a metaphor for living at God's direction and following in God's ways. Abraham, for example, is called by God to 'walk before me and be blameless' (Gen. 17:1) and the Christians in Rome are instructed by Paul to 'walk according to the Spirit' (Rom. 8:4, RSV). It is a figure of speech that provides a picture of steady, patient, step-by-step progress in an ongoing journey of faith, a journey that lasts a lifetime and constantly takes us through boundaries we thought we would never be able to cross. If Jonah's journey to Nineveh was long and arduous, our journeys as the people of God will be just as demanding, in spiritual, practical, emotional and cultural terms, if we want to reach *our* cities with the gospel. If we fail to make those journeys, we will be failing to walk with God.

For some of us, reaching the city still involves a literal journey to dark places where the social and economic gap between the privileged majority and the deprived minority in our nation is stark and shocking. Gary Bishop has been inspired by William Booth's book *In Darkest England and the Way Out*, published in 1891, in which he outlined his bold and innovative plans to lift people out of poverty. With a deliberate irony, Booth proposed his 'Cab Horse Charter' in which he stated that 'when a horse is down he is helped up, and while he lives he has food, shelter and work'. Booth asked for nothing less than this for the poorest people in our inner cities. But, despite his admiration for Booth and his commitment to serve in the part of the church which he founded, Gary has been sufficiently astute to discern a significant deficiency in Booth's commendable scheme for the poor

> Towards the end of *In Darkest England and the Way Out*, as Booth is summarising his thesis, he says that the reason that The Salvation Army is best placed to deliver the incredible plan that he has laid out is because many early day Salvationists were from these places. 'They are in touch with them. They live in the same street, work in the same shops and factories, and come in contact with them at every turn and corner of life.' One of the unique things about the Army was that it recruited many of its members and officers from the submerged tenth, the under classes. It took people who were uneducated and unskilled, in many cases addicted, destitute people and gave them hope and something to live for. Booth was right that it would be of huge benefit when trying to reach out to poor people in poor communities for the majority of your workforce to be familiar with that lifestyle. This would surely make access to people, relationship building and credibility much more achievable than if he had approached the same task with personnel primarily recruited from the middle and upper classes. However, I can't help feeling that, for all the genius of Booth's proposal, there is a weakness here in his long term thinking; shortly after he claims that many of his people are from the slums he says 'If they don't live

amongst them, they formerly did.' Presumably, having found salvation in Booth's Army, many had lifted themselves clear of their former lives and out of darkest England altogether. He would, of course, see this as positive progress and betterment for the individual and who could argue with that? The unemployed finding work, the alcoholic giving up the drink, the hungry being fed, the homeless being housed. But over time this process, repeated thousands of times, generation after generation, would result in the whole Army being upwardly mobile, upwards and away from the people it was first called to.[26]

Discerning a weakness is one thing; having the courage to do something about it is another. But that is just what Gary and a group of young adults did in 2000 when, under the umbrella of The Salvation Army and the Message Trust, they moved into one of the neediest areas in East Manchester, each of them committing to live there for a minimum of three years, to set up one of the city's Eden projects.

Darkest England and the Way Back In is more than just the title of Gary's moving and challenging record of life in the inner city; it is also an accurate description of the style of life and mission they are modelling for all who will take notice. From its beginnings as an exclusively youth venture, Eden Openshaw has evolved into an inner city church addressing itself to a wide variety of needs and problems. More than seven years later, Gary and his wife Hannah (now with a young family) and the nucleus of the original team are still there. Some have moved on to establish similar ministries in other parts of the city, continuing the journey into an environment and a culture which first shocked and amazed them. Gary is honest enough to confess just how unprepared he was for life in the inner city

You do not have to live in darkest England for long before
you realise who you are and where you come from.
Within a few short weeks of living in the inner city I
became acutely aware that I have had an immensely privileged upbringing . . . Like most of us, I have always pre-
sumed that my experience of life is the benchmark for
normality. My childhood memories of a loving family
with hard-working parents, holidays, comfortable houses,
clean clothes and the mouth-watering aroma of mum's
cooking filling the house every evening are nothing more
than a dream to the native children of my new community. Worse than that, as a child of this community your
personal safety cannot be guaranteed; the levels of violence behind the closed doors of private homes and in
public spaces mean that, inevitably, innocent bystanders
get caught in the crossfire. At a kids' club New Year party
we asked a child, 'Did you enjoy Christmas?' and her
response was a poignant reminder of just how unfamiliar
this land is to me: 'My Mum's boyfriend smashed a mir-
ror over my Mum's head so we spent most of it in hospi-
tal.' A far cry from the cosy, indulgent celebrations of my
childhood with open fires and dusty LPs sounding out
their sentimental festive tunes.[27]

Whether or not we are called to make that literal journey
and to relocate to the more deprived parts of our cities,
many of our Christian churches and congregations have
long and difficult paths to follow if they are to avoid
becoming isolated cultural and religious islands in the
neighbourhoods in which they are situated. Perhaps the
most pertinent question that can be asked of any leader
and any congregation is this: 'What difference would it
make to the surrounding community if your church
ceased to exist tomorrow?' Sadly and more often than
we would wish, the honest answer is 'Not much.'

We need to make the journey *from marketing to mission*. Certainly we have benefited from the insights of seeker-friendly churches that have come to us from North America. It is no bad thing to ask whether our worship is meaningful to the person attending for the first time and if the words we use and the music we employ are such that non-Christians can relate to what is happening. We do not commend the gospel by making it obscure and inaccessible. It is essential to make guests feel at home. There is nothing wrong with the philosophy of Willow Creek Church in Chicago that 'church should be a safe place to hear a dangerous message.' But seeker-friendly churches work best in a culture in which people still look on church attendance as a normal part of life for ordinary people, and where their family may have stopped attending in their own life-time or that of their parents. It is a marketing-based strategy, built around the concept of making the product better in order to attract the potential audience who have at least some predisposition to buy in.

But it doesn't go far enough in secularised, post-modern Britain where a significant proportion of families have not attended church for five or six generations. They barely know that church exists and what they do know simply confirms their suspicions that it is a minority pastime for a section of the population who have a peculiar interest in that sort of thing. The steady decline of main-line denominations – many of which have valiantly made a succession of attempts to tighten their administrative structures, to brighten up their image, and to take on board the latest idea for growth being touted – is clear evidence that a marketing approach will not work. A strategy based on improvement and invitation inevitably pushes us towards the same old default question: 'How do we get people to come to church?'

It is time to face two truths that we have avoided for too long: firstly, for the most part, they are not going to make that journey; it is too far from where they are and they don't even know where the path is any longer. But secondly and even more importantly, the imperative of the gospel is not that we should ask them to come to us, but that we should go to them. Improvement and invitation will still have a place, but they will be secondary to incarnation and involvement – learning to share the lives of those with whom we want to share Jesus.

That, in fact, is the very heart of mission, a word whose root meaning is 'to go': taking the church, and the ministry of the church, and – most important of all – the Lord of the church to where people are. When we do that we often discover that he is there already, waiting for us to catch up with him in the world outside the doors of the church. How that will look in practice will take many forms. It might be that, like the team in East Manchester, we physically move into a neighbourhood; it might mean establishing a small fellowship in our home; it might mean beginning an Alpha group in a local pub or leisure centre; it might mean, as in the case of one brave young man I know, beginning a low-key ministry among the 'goths' and 'moshers' who congregate in the city centre, befriending them and helping them find premises in which to rehearse their music, but doing it with all the grace and love of Christ so that our very presence commends the gospel and provokes questions as to why we do it. It might mean any of those and a thousand more imaginative ways of taking Jesus to wherever people are. But, unless such ministries exist alongside more traditional expressions of church, we will effectively disenfranchise large sections of our communities from hearing and responding to the gospel.

We need to make the journey *from closed shop to open house*. In effect, this means that it is imperative that we care less about building formal membership than encouraging authentic discipleship. That is implicit in all we have said in an earlier chapter about the importance of people being allowed to belong in order to believe. Open house churches will emphasise active participation over membership registration. (As one articulate young church planter said to me recently, 'Church for us today is more about joining in than joining up.') They will be messy and untidy places compared with those that many of us have grown up with. The challenge for the leaders of such open Christian communities will not be to make the decisions as to 'who's in and who's out' in terms of membership; rather, it will be to discern the *direction* in which people are heading spiritually and to pastor and minister to them accordingly. The question constantly on their minds will be: 'Are they making the journey towards commitment to following Christ, or are they drifting in the opposite direction?'

Open house churches will teach the word and train their people in Christian living by a combination of direct proclamation and shared exploration. A strong biblical authority in teaching gospel truth will go hand in hand with a flexible and intentional liberty in allowing open and honest questioning. In whatever form of small group is appropriate to the immediate context, they will provide maximum opportunity for seekers to express their doubts and acknowledge their difficulties in faith and practice. Recognising that an entire generation has now grown up in a multi-media culture, they will learn to communicate through the arts and symbolic actions as much as by the spoken and written word. Such churches will need to be *solid at the core*, led by men and women of deep Christian conviction, strong pastoral compassion, and with a willingness to embrace all the education and training they can access; at the same time, they will be *fuzzy at the edges*, allowing people to enter without the imposition of any conditions and to be as involved as they wish with the minimum of restriction.

For many leaders this will mean that need to travel a route that will be as demanding as Jonah's long trek to Nineveh. They will need to go all the way *from being caretakers to becoming risk-takers*. In years past, congregations demanded some very specific things of their leaders: they were expected to *pastor the flock*, visiting people in their homes and sometimes becoming more like a sheepdog than a shepherd; to *preserve the denominational traditions*, demonstrating their grasp of and adherence to the theological, behavioural and cultural norms of their denomination or church stream; and to *preside over the rites of passage*, conducting marriages, dedications of babies, and funerals – matching, hatching and dispatching, as it is often expressed colloquially!

To a greater or lesser extent, elements of these roles will always be part of a church leader's responsibilities. But there will be less and less need for those who are content to be custodians of denominational traditions. The nature of city life means that there is a need for leaders who will be *managers of change*, discerning the trends and movements of society and helping the people of God to adapt and apply the gospel in a time of unprecedented and rapid transition; leaders who will be *missiologists*, committed to the study and practice of leading the church to engage with the wider community in sacrificial service, meaningful dialogue and effective evangelism; leaders who will be *masters of strategy*, casting vision and setting goals that will translate God's agenda for his people into practical steps that allow every

member of the Body of Christ to play their part in taking
the church forward; and leaders who will be *merchants of
spiritual commerce*, able to sense the needs and fears of
the age in which we live, and to demonstrate the relevance and power of the gospel to meet every genuine
human longing.

The thought of such a spiritual and emotional journey
is enough to daunt the stoutest heart. But, as anyone
who has ever run a marathon knows, you complete the
race not by worrying about running twenty-six miles;
that would simply be too much for all but the elite ath-
letes; the secret is to concentrate on running one mile at
a time, and to repeat that twenty-six times. It's amazing
how many ordinary runners can do that. It will be no
less amazing what we can do to reach our Nineveh step
by step.

Eight

Transforming the city

Learning the lessons

One afternoon in the spring of 1928, the young jazz tenor saxophonist, Bud Freeman, was walking with a fellow musician through the neighbourhood where he lived in South Side Chicago. Despite the fact that the other man was only a few years older than he was, Freeman was in considerable awe of his companion. As they turned a corner, they chanced on a group of street musicians giving a very second-rate rendition of a tune that had been recently released on gramophone record with the splendid title, *Struttin' with some barbecue*. The trumpet player, who had obviously listened to it over and over again, struggled to play the solo note for note from the record.

When, to the relief of his listeners, he had finished, Freeman's companion nonetheless applauded politely. Then, not wishing to embarrass the trumpet player, he sidled up to him and whispered in his ear, 'Man, you're playing that too *slow*.' Taken aback by this unsolicited advice, he asked somewhat tetchily, 'How would *you* know?' 'Because,' came the reply, 'I'm Louis Armstrong. That's my chorus you're playing.'

A suitably chastened trumpet player listened attentively and gratefully to a little further musical tuition
from the great man. The next day Freeman and
Armstrong took the same route through the city and,
sure enough, the street buskers were in the same spot
playing the same tune with just the slightest hint of an
improvement on the part of the trumpet player.
However, there was one big difference from the previous
day. Now, propped up against their tin collecting cup
was a hand-written notice which proudly announced,
'Pupils of Louis Armstrong.'

Jazz historians have commented many times that
everyone who has ever tried to play the music is, in
some sense, a pupil of Louis Armstrong. That's not to
say that those who followed him have been content to
play the same tunes in the same way as their mentor.
There's a big difference between learning from someone
and slavish imitation. If you listen to Wynton Marsalis,
for example, with any understanding of the musical tradition in which he stands, you will recognise the unmistakable influence of Armstrong. But you will also be
aware that because he has a different personality,
expressing his art at a different place and time, the
music, too, is inevitably different.

The point of our story – apart from the worthy cause
of educating as many readers as possible in the greatest
art form that God ever gave to the world! – is this: the
story of Jonah, like the rest of the Bible, has been recorded, not primarily to satisfy our historical curiosity, but
to teach us the great lessons we need to guide us in our
belief and our behaviour. That doesn't mean that we
respond – as some have mistakenly tried to do – by slav-
ishly seeking to emulate every practice recorded in the
Bible and imagining that in so doing we are being obedient to Scripture. If we pushed that idea to its logical

conclusion we would all still be wearing sandals and robes and speaking Hebrew, Aramaic or New Testament Greek. Instead it means that we have to do the sometimes difficult work of what scholars call *hermeneutics*, interpreting the meaning of a passage of Scripture, setting it in its historical context, extracting its principles, and then applying it to the time and culture in which we find ourselves. The wonderfully told story of Jonah's evangelistic campaign in Nineveh presents us with a great challenge and a perfect opportunity to do just that. If we fail to interpret the text for our time, we will find ourselves persuading the nation's farmers to force their livestock to wear sackcloth and observe days of fasting. And one suspects that would be counter-productive in seeking to share the gospel.

Telling the whole truth

Then the word of the LORD came to Jonah a second time: "Go to the great city of Nineveh and proclaim to it the message I give you."

Jonah obeyed the word of the LORD and went to Nineveh. Now Nineveh was a very important city – a visit required three days. On the first day, Jonah started into the city. He proclaimed: "Forty more days and Nineveh will be overturned."

(Jon. 3:1–4)

The writer of Jonah is a master of the short story genre. We have already recognised the vein of humour that runs through the narrative. Now we need to be alert to the subtle verbal nuances as the tale moves towards its climax: little differences that invite us to take note of what is happening both to Nineveh and to Jonah. When the word of the Lord comes for a second time, the task is essentially the same: deliver God's message to the people of Nineveh. But Jonah is different; he's been exposed to storms at sea, pagans who pray, a fish who swallows prophets, and, above all, a God whose relentless pursuit of his reluctant spokesman is matched only by his infinite patience in seeking to overcome Jonah's prejudice and offer him a second chance. Surely his own experience of God's undeserved favour will inspire him to deliver the message of God's impending judgement with rather more grace than he might have done originally.

And, as if to underline the change of tone, God's command to Jonah is phrased very differently from what it had been originally. In the opening sentence of chapter one, the call had been stark and to the point: 'Go to the great city of Nineveh and preach against it, because its wickedness has come up before me.' Now there is a softening in the phraseology, a hint that God may have something more in mind than judgement alone: 'Go to the great city of Nineveh and proclaim to it the message I give you.' Tantalisingly, the content of the message is not spelt out for us, but we should recall that the last words we heard from the lips of Jonah, just before his abrupt exit from the fish's belly, were a declaration of faith in a God who is ultimately more concerned about deliverance than punishment: 'Salvation comes from the LORD.' It would hardly be presumptuous for us to assume that this new emphasis will be reflected in his message.

Even the word 'message' in God's instruction to Jonah has a significance we cannot ignore, especially in the light of the New Testament. The Septuagint (the name comes from the Latin word for 'seventy' and is derived from the Jewish tradition that the work was completed by seventy-two scholars in seventy-two days) was a Greek translation of the Old Testament made for the use of Greek-speaking Jews. It was in common use in the first century AD and many of the Old Testament quotations in the New Testament are taken from the Septuagint. In that translation, the Hebrew word for 'message' is translated by the Greek word *kerygma*. It literally means 'the proclamation of a herald' and it came to have a very particular meaning in the New Testament where it was used to describe the content of the apostles' foundational teaching in the early church.

When scholars have sought to analyse the 'kerygma' of the early church, several elements stand out

- Jesus is the fulfilment of Old Testament prophecy in his life, death and resurrection
- as the Risen Lord he now sits at the right hand of his Father
- the presence of the Holy Spirit in the church is the evidence and sign of this
- God's plan will reach its ultimate consummation in the return of Jesus Christ as Lord and judge
- in the light of these truths, there is opportunity to repent and to find forgiveness and salvation through Jesus.

It is a glorious proclamation of truth that leaves the hearer in no doubt as to the power and authority of God but which ultimately emphasises his mercy and his desire for all to find forgiveness.

Of course, Jonah lived centuries before God's complete revelation of his grace through Jesus, so his message would obviously not have contained the full *kerygma* of the apostles in New Testament times. Nonetheless, it is not at all fanciful for us to conclude that his proclamation on that first day in Nineveh was more than just a warning of impending judgement from God, and that it presented a God who was more loving than angry. Even the brief record of his sermon, which on the surface seems to be no more than a prediction of impending doom, contains within it a hint of hope. If God's primary agenda was to wipe out the city, why bother with the warning, 'Forty more days and Nineveh will be overturned'? At the very least, the Ninevites were being given some time to reflect on their present course and to consider how they might respond to this message.

But again there seems to be deliberate ambivalence in Jonah's words which we miss in our English translation. The Hebrew word *hapak* which is translated as 'overthrown' in English is undoubtedly a word that speaks of fierce judgement. It is used three times in close succession in the Genesis story of God's terrible destruction of Sodom and Gomorrah (Gen. 19:21,25,29) so Jewish readers would have been in no doubt that God meant business with a people who wilfully flaunted his commands. But they would also have known that the word has another, more positive shade of meaning. The same word is used of Saul when he is dramatically altered for good by an encounter with a band of prophets (1 Sam. 10:6) and it is used again in Deuteronomy to describe how God intervenes to turn a curse into a blessing (Deut. 23:5). The nature of Nineveh's overturning might be her destruction; but, equally so, it might be a complete God-inspired turnaround in the city's values and attitudes. It all hinges on their response to Jonah's message.

Before we face the challenge of what this means for us today, it will be helpful to note one more thing about Jonah's *kerygma* and particularly how it was delivered. It is not difficult to imagine how the prophet must have been feeling when he began to speak. The long journey probably left him at a point of exhaustion, his nervousness and fear must have caused his knees to knock and his voice to quaver, and it would hardly be surprising if there was a hint of embarrassment on his face as he inwardly acknowledged his delay in arriving in the city with his summons to repentance. No matter. It would have been a great improvement on his likely attitude to the Ninevites before his experience of God's relentless pursuit and saving grace. And perhaps the truth is that tough messages are best delivered by frail messengers. Then the hearers are in no doubt as to where the power really lies. Paul acknowledges as much to the Corinthians about his own ministry

> When I came to you, brothers, I did not come with eloquence or superior wisdom as I proclaimed to you the testimony about God. For I resolved to know nothing while I was with you except Jesus Christ and him crucified. I came to you in weakness and fear, and with much trembling. My message and my preaching were not with wise and persuasive words, but with a demonstration of the Spirit's power, so that your faith might not rest on men's wisdom, but on God's power (1 Cor. 2:1–5).

And here's the point of this prolonged excavation beneath the surface of our story in order to mine its deeper meaning. The task of the church is still to deliver God's message, unadulterated and unchanged. That message will always and inevitably contain an element of judgement as a holy God stands before a world in which oppression, injustice, hunger, homelessness, poverty and the ravages of war still afflict millions of our fellow human beings. We fail in our duty as heralds of the *kerygma*, if we do not bring the warning of God's justice and certain punishment if we do not repent. But there are three things we must keep in mind in delivering that message.

Firstly, we need to draw a lesson from the fact that Jonah's message was delivered to the city and not just to a few individuals on whom he happened to hit because he found their particular sins to be especially distasteful to him. We are not told the content of his message, but it's reasonable to assume that he addressed himself at least as much to issues of institutional violence, corporate sin and structural injustice as to the subject of personal morality. Too often we are selective in the sins we choose to denounce, focussing primarily on aspects of personal behaviour and sometimes, it seems, exclusively on matters of sexual conduct. It isn't that these things are not important or that we should hold back from modelling and encouraging high standards of personal behaviour. It's simply that there is a temptation to focus on them to the exclusion of everything else.

To take an obvious example, in recent years the church seems to have had an undue and even unhealthy preoccupation with matters of gay sexuality. We must have used up entire rain forests with the documents and statements we have issued on this subject. The end result of all this has not been a turning towards heterosexual marriage. Instead, we have simply managed to convince large sections of the gay community that we are angry with them, that we don't like them, and that the Christian church is the last place they should look for support and unconditional acceptance. That has left us far short of the attitude of Jesus who always seems to have had a particular understanding of and tenderness towards those who were guilty of sexual sin. It also means that we have used up spiritual, emotional and political capital that would have been more profitably expended asking why governments can spend billions of dollars on military hardware to wage war in oil-rich countries while doing little or nothing about hunger and genocide in a number of African states.

Secondly, the over-arching characteristics of our message must always be hope for the future and the promise of God's love and forgiveness. As we reminded ourselves in chapter Two, this world is fallen and flawed; in some places it is desperately sick and sinful; and it is, to use C.S. Lewis's phrase, 'enemy-occupied territory' – the presence of evil is too obvious to be doubted or ignored. But it is still *God's world*; he offers hope and forgiveness to all who will turn to him and it is our task to make that clear to all. If we have a duty to faithfully declare God's judgement, then we have an even greater responsibility to extravagantly and joyfully dispense God's grace to all kinds and conditions of people, and to do it in both word and action. No one is beyond redemption; we must demonstrate that by our loving words and our eager willingness to embrace and accept people into our fellowship, irrespective of their race, gender, social status, sexual orientation or past history. And no situation is beyond hope; we must demonstrate that in our public pronouncements and our readiness to be involved in serving in the areas of greatest need.

Thirdly, we must heed the counsel implicit both in Paul's testimony to the manner in which we brought the gospel *kerygma* to Corinth and in Jonah's lonely stance in the streets of Nineveh. The humility and authenticity of the messenger allowed the clarity of God's message and the authority of God's Spirit to work together to elicit a response from the hearer. Both are very far removed from the stereotypical image of the slick-talking, expensively dressed, jewellery-draped evangelist of television fame; both are very different from the angry preacher whose chief purpose in life appears to be to denounce every innocent human pastime; both are completely unlike the caricature of the omni-competent Christian leader who never sinned or made a mistake. The hard fact – and, indeed, the encouraging truth – is that an extraordinary message of grace always needs to be delivered by ordinary men and women who are themselves living examples of that grace at work in slowly transforming human lives.

Reaching the whole city

The Ninevites believed God. They declared a fast, and all of them, from the greatest to the least, put on sackcloth.

When the news reached the king of Nineveh, he rose from his throne, took off his royal robes, covered himself with sackcloth and sat down in the dust. Then he issued a proclamation in Nineveh:

'By the decree of the king and his nobles:

Do not let any man or beast, herd or flock, taste anything; do not let them eat or drink. But let man and beast be covered with sackcloth. Let everyone call urgently on God. Let them give up their evil ways and their violence. Who knows? God may yet relent and with compassion turn from his fierce anger so that we will not perish.'   (Jon. 3:5–9)

You wouldn't know whether to laugh or cry at this point: it's just so unfair. The run-away prophet, the narrow-minded, small-town preacher from Gath-Hepher, is the most successful evangelist in history, the only man to have a 100 per cent response to his appeal. *The entire city believes God*. From the king in the palace to the cattle out in the pasture, they fast and put on sackcloth as a sign of their mourning and repentance. It must have been a remarkable sight. But again, behind the undoubted humour with which the story is told and beneath the unfamiliar culture in which the story is set, there are principles which are relevant to mission in the twenty-first century.

When God presents Jonah with his assignment at the beginning of the first and third chapter, he refers on both occasions to 'the great city of Nineveh.' That repeated phrase is highly significant. God is concerned both for the people of Nineveh and the city itself; and, unlike many contemporary models of evangelism, Jonah was clearly not preaching just for individual decisions; he was not content to win a few conversions and leave things in the city of Nineveh just as they were before. His message constituted a call to the radical transformation of an entire society – 'Nineveh will be overturned' – and, as such, it anticipated the message of Jesus himself who began his ministry by announcing the coming of the Kingdom, the rule and reign of God over every area of life.

We, too, are called to impact our cities, to be salt and light, penetrating and purifying every human activity. The proclamation of the whole gospel to the whole city in our generation will demand that individual Christians are fully involved in the life of the city, expressing their concern by focussed prayer and active participation in politics and community initiatives and events. That will mean that often they will need to be released from an over-concentration on attending and maintaining purely church activities. Of course, it will always be important that Christians give proper time to meeting for worship, prayer, the study of the Bible, and the vital spiritual work of building each other up in the faith. But we will need to ask which activities really do serve those purposes and which amount to little more than maintaining the machinery of the church. Too many churches are still programme-driven, and too many of those programmes do little to deepen the spiritual life of the members or benefit the community.

Impacting our cities also means that local churches will continue to demonstrate their commitment to the wider community in practical service such as parent and toddler clubs, activities for children and teenagers, family events, care for the elderly or the lonely, and ministry to the poor and the marginalised. Indeed, it would be churlish not to recognise the tremendous amount of good work that takes place in such initiatives every day. Our cities would be much the poorer if churches suddenly withdrew their labour on behalf of those who are not members.

But even those good things are not enough by themselves. It is instructive to note that the 'overturning' of Nineveh really began to gain momentum from the moment the king himself was drawn into what was happening. In fact, he is the one who spells out the specifics of repentance for his people. They had already decided to fast and put on sackcloth in response to Jonah's message. But the challenge to 'give up their evil ways and their violence' comes not from the prophet but from the King. Jonah had God's authority to declare the word of judgement and mercy; the king had God's authority to translate that word into practical and specific policies. And, despite the sinfulness of the city, a sinfulness for which its leaders were as much responsible as its citizens, the king has a genuine compassion for his people and is anxious to do all he can so that God will relent of his anger and the city will not perish.

This is a lesson which much of the church still has to learn. If we are going to turn our cities around, it is essential that we learn how to relate to and dialogue with those who are the leaders and opinion-formers in our society – politicians at national and local level, leaders in business and commerce, influential figures in the arts and the world of sport and entertainment, professionals in the fields of health care and education, and those who wield the persuasive power of the media. We are foolish and even arrogant if we fail to acknowledge that there are many men and women of goodwill in public life who, though they make no profession of faith, are doing a great deal for the benefit of others. And we will limit the power of the gospel to change our cities if we do not learn to work with them.

In order to do that, we need to get our own house in order. The good work of local churches of every size and of all streams and denominations must be augmented by the church speaking, as far as possible, with a united voice that civic leaders and others can hear and respond to. That means that in every town and city, church leaders must be willing to do the hard and often painful work of strengthening and developing structures and relationships that will allow us to make representations on major issues to statutory bodies and powerful groups in the community. (It is surprising how often we are content just to plough our own furrow and neglect our responsibilities to the wider church. Could it be that there are times when we are guilty of building and guarding our own kingdom?)

This is not to suggest for one moment that we should try to become a kind of 'moral majority.' That would be disastrous. If it is true that power tends to corrupt, it is even more the case that nothing becomes as corrupt as the church when it seeks to hold power. God did not bring his church into being for that purpose and, consequently, when we try to take power we handle it very badly. We were created for something that is ultimately far stronger than power; we were created for influence. And one of the greatest tasks facing us is to learn how to exercise that influence to the full.

It has been an enormous privilege to be part of the church in Manchester for more than seven years. It certainly isn't that the church here is perfect, but rather that we have begun to learn how to work together in order to bless and speak to our city. Part of this has been a city-wide prayer movement whose leaders make it their business to let those in positions of civic authority know that we are praying for them, to ask them what we should pray for and, when appropriate, to invite them to attend our prayer events. It was both deeply moving and enormously encouraging to see the city's first Muslim Lord Mayor attend a Christian prayer gathering without any embarrassment on his part and without any inappropriate or insensitive evangelism on the part of his hosts. We were able to acknowledge together that God cares about the great city of Manchester just as much as he did about the great city of Nineveh.

That same concern for the city has involved us in dialogue with civic leaders on major issues such as gambling and the proposed new super-casino that is now coming to the city. That provided a good example of how the church can participate. It meant that the Christian representation had to be made alongside that of other religious faiths, whose concerns were as genuine as ours and whose moral convictions were very similar to ours. It was imperative that we had done our research and knew our facts. (Nothing damages our credibility more than well-meaning Christians who don't know what they're talking about.) It also meant that we had to balance our integrity with the fact that our view-point was not the only one and that a level of practical compromise would be inevitable. As people of faith, we could not endorse major gambling outlets because of our shared conviction that it is an industry with a moral flaw at its centre and our concern for those problem-gamblers for whom it is as addictive as any illegal drug. But we also had to accept that our position might not win the day and work towards ensuring that, if and when the casino was approved, proper constraints and controls were put in place. The end result is not all that we would have wanted, but it is a good deal better than if we had remained aloof from the process. We have, at least, added a little salt to the mix and shed a little more light in the darkness.

It may all seem a long way from kings issuing proclamations decreeing city-wide fasting and cows wearing sackcloth in response to a street-preacher who has just walked nine hundred miles to deliver his message. But the challenge of reaching our cities is as real today as it was for Jonah and the principles for meaningful engagement remain the same. Thankfully, the extravagant grace of God is real and unchanged too. The question Jonah and we must now face is just how close our hearts and our attitudes are to his.

Nine

The big issues

My wife was at home suffering from a rare bout of flu and the car was in the garage suffering from one its much more frequent breakdowns. So, as a dutiful husband, I had collected some essential groceries from the corner-shop with the help of a list dictated by my spouse from her sick-bed. As normally happens to men, I'd had extreme difficulty in locating the items on the shelves. Indeed, I had half-convinced myself that a malicious shop assistant had spotted me coming along the road and had swiftly and randomly rearranged the items just to afford some free entertainment for her colleagues. I left the shop laden down with what seemed like enough groceries to feed a family three times the size of ours and with the air of a man who knows he has gone far beyond the reasonable call of duty.

But few things lift the clouds of gloom quicker than being able to commiserate with a fellow-sufferer, and I was glad to fall into step with another harassed-looking man trudging homewards with his shopping bags. Our conversation was easy and amiable and we talked about the things that men talk about – the horror of shopping, the pleasure of football and the failure of human ingenuity to devise and produce a car that a man could actually rely on when he most needed it. And before I had even realised it, we reached our front gate. We thanked each other for our company and my companion in adversity made to continue along the road.

It was then I made my big mistake. I remembered my sermon the previous week exhorting the congregation to be alert to every opportunity to share their faith, to gossip the gospel, and to invite others to church. Here was my opportunity to model it for them and to share my success in an up-to-date sermon illustration the following Sunday. Who knows, my new-found friend might well be in the front row to provide living proof of my evangelistic prowess. 'By the way,' I said, trying to sound as casual and matter-of-fact as I could, 'I lead The Salvation Army church in town. It's a great congregation. You'd be really welcome any Sunday.' The look on his face will remain etched on my memory until my dying day. He put his shopping bags on the ground, paused just long enough to compose himself, and said, 'Listen, mate, I've got enough problems. My wife's left me, I'm bringing up the kids on my own, and I've just lost my job. And you want to add religion to all that. Don't you think I've got enough on my plate?' And with that he shook his head in disbelief, picked up his shopping bags, and hurried along the road without so much as a backwards glance, obviously intent on making good his escape from the religious maniac he'd just encountered.

That little incident took place more years ago than I care to remember, but it taught me a lesson I will not easily forget. Religion has a bad press. For most people it's the biggest turn-off imaginable. That's why the vast majority of those who work beside us and who live next door to us attend church, if at all, only for weddings, christenings, funerals, and at Christmas. And it can't *all* be their fault. There must be something wrong with the way in which we have communicated and represented the gospel which, we claim, brings life in all its fullness. Is there anything we can learn from the story of Jonah? Why did the people of Nineveh respond so whole-heartedly to his message? What does it tell us about the nature of the faith we must exercise, about the character of the universe in which we live, and about the dangers of the religion we profess?

The nature of faith

> **The Ninevites believed God. They declared a fast, and all of them, from the greatest to the least, put on sack-cloth . . .**
> **". . . Who knows? God may yet relent and with com-passion turn from his fierce anger so that we will not perish."** (Jon. 3:5,9)

Whatever Jonah's skills as a preacher might have been, one thing is clear: he certainly didn't have time to edu-cate the people of Nineveh in sound doctrine and deep theological truths. All he could do was to warn them that their present way of life was not pleasing to God and that, one way or another, things were about to be shaken up. And yet they threw themselves on the mercy of God – every last man, woman and beast in the city. Scholars and historians have speculated on what objective cause might have brought the city to its knees in such immedi-ate mass repentance. Had they been defeated in battle? Had there been some internal civil strife? Had the city been afflicted by some natural disaster such as flooding or famine? Had there been some astrological abnormality, a solar eclipse perhaps? Any of these might have been interpreted as a sign of divine disapproval and the citizens of Nineveh might have been ripe for repentance. If that was the case, then part of the miracle of God's intervention in the history of the city might simply have been the timing of Jonah's visit.

Whether any of those things actually occurred and whether they served to make Jonah's hearers more receptive to his message than would otherwise have been the case, we will never be sure. What is more important for us to understand is that, whatever the circumstances that sensitised their hearts and minds to Jonah's words, 'the Ninevites believed God' – nothing more and nothing less than that. The biblical record does not concern itself with the fact that they were pagans whose primary religious allegiance was to Ishtar, the goddess of fertility, love and war. Nor does it inform us how or even whether their religious worship changed from that day forward. When we are told that they 'believed God', we are learning simply that they threw themselves on the mercy of Yahweh, the God of Israel, whom Jonah served and whose message he declared.

Their belief meant not that they had fully understood or that they were certain beyond any doubt that Jonah's announcement of judgement and his offer of grace were secure. The king's decree articulates their combination of questioning and hope: 'Who knows? God may yet turn from his fierce anger so that we will not perish.' Belief for the people of Nineveh – and it was enough to ensure their salvation – was simply the willingness to risk everything on the mercy of a just but loving God. At the heart of this very brief but incredibly bold drama is the daring declaration that all any of us can ultimately do in relation to God – whether we are devotees of pagan gods, monotheistic Jews, born-again Christians, devout followers of any of the world's other religions, sceptical agnostics or hardened atheists – is to acknowledge our unworthiness and risk everything on the one bet worth making: that God is infinitely good, extravagantly generous, and unceasingly willing to forgive and accept us.

What we learn in Jonah is nothing other than what we learn throughout the Bible. Early in the Old Testament, when God calls him from his home in Haran to embark on a journey that will lead him to a new land and to be the founder of a great nation, Abraham remains far from perfect, as even a cursory reading of his story in Genesis will quickly reveal. But the verdict on Abraham as a righteous man is based not on his conduct but on his willingness to risk everything on God's word: 'Abram believed the LORD, and he credited it to him as righteousness' (Gen. 15:6). And that same theme is taken up and becomes the great rallying cry of Paul in the New Testament. The death of Jesus, he insists, was far more than a tragic accident, far more than a terrible injustice, far more than a meaningless act of Roman judicial violence. It was, in fact, a demonstration of God's love in which he took upon himself all the suffering and sin of the world and transformed it into an act of deliverance. We are all by nature part of the world's problem and all we can do, just as the Ninevites did, is to risk everything, make the bet with our very lives, and throw ourselves on the mercy of a God who loves to the extent of the cross.

The objection that has always been made to this kind of faith is that it isn't fair, it lets us off the hook, it makes no distinction between the good and the bad, no differentiation between the deserving and the undeserving. That was part of Jonah's argument with God. Nineveh was an evil place full of evil people who didn't deserve to be delivered. Jonah and his kin, on the other hand, were good and God should stick with them. What it fails to take account of is the fact that we are all like the man in Jesus' joke: 'Why do you look at the speck of sawdust in your brother's eye and pay no attention to the plank in your own eye?' (Mt. 7:3). It's a neat one-liner with an enormous lesson for those willing to listen and reflect. We all have defective moral and spiritual vision; none of us can see the complete truth about ourselves, who and what we really are; none of us appreciates that we are every bit as flawed, and often more so, than our neighbour; none of us has a full grasp of truth. The best, indeed the only thing, we can do is to trust that God loves us and will accept us as we are.

The character of the universe

> When God saw what they did and how they turned from their evil ways, he had compassion and did not bring upon them the destruction he had threatened.
> (Jon. 3:10)

When we reach this point in our story, it is impossible to avoid the issue of the kind of universe we live in. For the author of Jonah, as for all the biblical writers, *human choices have meaning and human actions have consequences*. In terms of vocabulary, those are simple statements; but in terms of human morality and spirituality, they express the most profound truths. And they are truths that derive from the nature of our loving Creator-God, from the freedom he confers upon us as human beings made in his image, and from the relationship with himself for which he created us.

Just how important those truths are to our understanding of human life and dignity can best be seen if we
set them against the prevailing philosophy that the universe and humanity are merely the result of blind
chance. There are many who hold to this position, but
noone has ever expressed it more starkly or more elo-
quently than Jacques Monod, the French molecular biol-
ogist and Nobel prize winner in the 1960s

> Chance alone is at the source of every innovation, of all
> creation in the biosphere. Pure chance, absolutely free but
> blind, at the very root of the stupendous edifice of evolu-
> tion: this central concept of modern biology is no longer
> one among other possible or even conceivable hypothe-
> ses. It is today the sole conceivable hypothesis . . .[28]

It is Monod's conviction that we must come to terms
with what this means for humankind, that we should
face the terrible truth about our relationship to the universe in which we find ourselves

> The universe was not pregnant with life nor the bio-
> sphere with man. Our number came up in a Monte Carlo
> game. Is it any wonder if, like the person who has just
> made a million at the casino, we feel strange and a little
> unreal . . . If he accepts this message – accepts all it con-
> tains – then man must at last wake out of his millenary
> dream; and in doing so, wake to his total solitude, his
> fundamental isolation. Now does he at last realise that,
> like a gipsy, he lives on the boundary of an alien world.
> A world that is deaf to his music, just as indifferent to his
> hopes as it is to his sufferings or his crimes.[29]

That is a deeply moving but intensely bleak view of
humanity. It means that life is pointless, that human

choices are meaningless, and that all our best efforts are ultimately without value or purpose. And it tends paradoxically to exert a pull in two seemingly opposite directions. Most obviously, it can draw people towards, or perhaps more accurately provide an excuse for, the kind of licence in behaviour described by the novelist and philosopher, Aldous Huxley

> The philosopher who finds no meaning in the world is not concerned exclusively with a problem in pure metaphysics; he is also concerned to prove that there is no valid reason why he personally should not do as he wants to do . . . For myself, as, no doubt, for most of my contemporaries, the philosophy of meaninglessness was essentially an instrument of liberation. The liberation we desired was simultaneously liberation . . . from a certain system of morality. We objected to the morality because it interfered with our sexual freedom; we objected to the political and economic system because it was unjust. The supporters of these systems claimed that in some way they embodied the meaning (a Christian meaning, they insisted) of the world. There was one admirably simple method of confuting these people and at the same time justifying ourselves in our political and erotic revolt: we could deny that the world had any meaning whatsoever . . .[30]

On the other hand, the belief that the entire universe, including human beings, is merely the result of 'blind chance' can create the intellectual soil in which a kind of behavioural determinism takes root. In a meaningless world which is the result of random forces, it is argued, human beings are no more than complex biological machines and their apparently free choices are really nothing more than the result of genetic and environmental factors. The behavioural psychologist, B.F. Skinner, whose best known book was significantly entitled *Beyond Freedom and Dignity*, is reputed to have said, 'I did not direct my life. I didn't design it. I never made decisions. Things always came up and made them for me. That's what life is.'

Now contrast these philosophies of life with the world-view that stands behind all that happens in the story of Jonah. Far from being a cosmic accident, the universe is the creation of a loving God who seeks our cooperation in his active concern for the world; human behaviour is not predetermined by environmental or genetic forces; human choices are real and significant and they will result either in our willing cooperation with God's plans or in our stubborn resistance to his purposes. Such convictions do not put us on a collision course with the findings of science. They simply recognise that, whereas the work of the scientist is to discover and explain how natural processes take place, science cannot address itself to the ultimate questions of the meaning of life. Those can be answered only by the different and deeper truths that are discovered and explored in an encounter with the living God.

The experiences of Jonah in his dealings with God bear witness to the truth that Christians know only too well: faith in God is not a convenient crutch for the emotionally and psychologically weaker members of the human race. An authentic encounter with the living God is not an easy option; it will prove to be far more costly than living for oneself. But it is infinitely preferable to the bleak alternatives that arise when we seek to live without God; and it is so challenging that sometimes even religion can be used as a hiding place from God rather than as an expression of devotion to him.

The danger of religion

> But Jonah was greatly displeased and became angry. He prayed to the LORD, "O LORD is this not what I said when I was still at home? That is why I was so quick to flee to Tarshish. I knew that you are a gracious and compassionate God, slow to anger and abounding in love, a God who relents from sending calamity. Now, O LORD, take away my life, for it is better for me to die than to live."   (Jon. 4:1–3)

By this point in the story it would be have been reasonable to assume that we could no longer be surprised by Jonah's narrow-minded prejudices. How wrong we would have been. His reaction to God's mercy towards Nineveh stands alongside the request of James and John, when they selfishly asked Jesus for the places of honour in his coming kingdom (Mk. 10:35–45), as one of the worst prayers ever made. It is a moment that is both comic and tragic. The prophet has just witnessed a 100 per cent response to his message; the entire city has repented. Any normal, self-respecting evangelist would be over the moon. Jonah, however is under a cloud, a dark cloud of depression. And the terrible truth comes pouring out in a torrent of vitriol.

We wouldn't have been surprised if he'd complained about the Ninevites being undeserving of God's mercy. We've already seen that unpleasant side of Jonah's character. But what comes out of his mouth and heart at this point is genuinely shocking. His reluctance to go to Nineveh, he confesses, arose from the very fact that he *knew* what God was like - gracious and compassionate, patient and slow to get angry, and 'abounding in love.' He knew all those things because they were part of one of Israel's great liturgical confessions of faith, part of the Scriptures, much of which he could probably recite by heart (Ex. 34:6,7). He knew that God was more likely to forgive than destroy the Ninevites, and he couldn't live with that truth. How is it possible that a prophet of Israel, a man charged with delivering the word of God, has reached a place where he cannot rejoice in – cannot even cope with – a God who is infinitely loving and merciful?

The answer is found in Jesus' beautiful but terrible story of the Father and his two sons, the story we call, not completely accurately, the parable of the prodigal son. It is a tale that is simple enough in its outline. A well-to-do farmer has two sons, the younger of whom, with all the impatience and ingratitude of youth, cannot wait for his father to die in order that he can inherit his portion of the estate. So he demands his share and takes himself off to a distant land where he fritters away his inheritance. At his lowest point, destitute and depressed, he comes to his senses, pockets his pride and heads for home, where he plans to acknowledge his unworthiness and ask his father to take him back as a hired servant. But his father sees him trudging along the road, runs to greet him with an embrace, restores him to his place in the family and throws a party to celebrate.

It's at this point that events take a very different course and the tone of the story changes dramatically. His older brother, returning from a day's hard work on his father's farm, hears the sound of the festivities and asks for an explanation. He greets the news of his brother's return not with joy but with anger. He protests that it isn't fair; he has served his father all these years and there was no party for him; so he's certainly not about to join the party for a wastrel he refuses even to call his brother. The hardness of the older son draws from the father a great and moving statement of the essence of the gospel: 'My son . . . you are always with me, and everything I have is yours. But we had to celebrate and be glad, because this brother of yours was dead and is alive again; he was lost and is found' (Lk: 15:31,32).

To repeat the question we asked about Jonah: how is it that the older son in Jesus' story is unable to rejoice at the return of his brother and his father's willingness to forgive? How is it that, despite a lifetime of faithful hard work, he totally fails to understand and share his father's heart? The answer is tragically obvious and unavoidable. The prophet Jonah and the hard-working brother have both succumbed to the danger of loveless religion. It is a fact of history and experience that religion has the capacity to be the best of things and the worst of things: the best of things because it provides a conduit through which human beings can channel their devotion to God; the worst of things because it can just as easily become a rigid system within which personal devotion to God can degenerate into hard-hearted self-righteousness or even self-deceiving hypocrisy.

The poet Robert Burns was himself a man of imperfect morals. But he possessed a unique ability to cut through pretence and hypocrisy with a penetrating accuracy that went straight to the heart of the matter. In *Holy Willie's Prayer* he paints a wickedly funny word picture of self-righteous religiosity that is certain of its own salvation and equally suspicious that just about everyone else is bound for hell. It is immediately recognisable even by those for whom lowland Scots is not their native dialect

> I bless and praise thy matchless might,
> When thousands thou hast left in night,
> That I am here before thy sight,
> For gifts and grace,

A burning and a shining light
To a' this place . . .

Yet I am here, a chosen sample,
To show thy grace is great and ample;
I'm here, a pillar o' thy temple
Strong as a rock,
A guide, a buckler and example
To a' thy flock.

O Lord, thou kens what zeal I bear,
When drinkers drink and swearers swear,
And singin' there and dancin' here
Wi' great and sma';
For I am keepet by thy fear,
Free frae them a' . . .[31]

The reader is not surprised when, after several verses like those above, Holy Willie is revealed to be somewhat less of 'a burning and a shining light' than he initially presents himself. Sadly, he is no mere figment of Burns's imagination, being based on a well-known character in the parish of Mauchline where the poet lived at that time. Nor are he and his kind confined to the pages of history; most of us have met his contemporary counterparts more often than we would have wished. It makes one wonder how many people have been kept from the fellowship of the church and held back from an encounter with God because of their experience of those whose religion knows nothing of the mercy of God and even less of the joy of a gospel which dispenses grace generously and extravagantly.

Indeed, there is an even more terrible side to religion than the smug self-righteousness that Burns satirises so devastatingly. Prejudice and bigotry, allied to the certainty that they alone possess the truth, have led religious people to perpetrate some of the most heinous of crimes over the centuries. The Crusades of the Middle Ages, the Spanish Inquisition and the Islamist terrorist bombings of our own time all bear witness to the dangers of religion that is divorced from the truths that we are all sinners deserving of divine judgement, that God in his love and mercy extends his grace to all, and that none of us is in sole or complete possession of the truth.

We will do well to remember Bill Hybel's dictum that the difference between the gospel and religion is simple: it's the way in which they are spelled. When asked what he means by that, he responds that religion is spelled *d-o*: it is about our achievements and what we have done for God, for ourselves and for others. The gospel, on the other hand, is spelled *d-o-n-e*: its emphasis is not on our good deeds but on the fact that God, in his love and mercy, has given his Son for our salvation. From the best to the worst of humankind, all that we can do is to accept his grace and mercy. When that happens, the focus of our lives shifts from doing our religious duty to allowing God to be God. And that is the last and greatest message of all in Jonah's story.

Ten

Let God be God

One of the characteristics of serious dramatists is that they never succumb to the temptation to sell out to the cliché of a happy ending. Their art is not about providing easy answers and wrapping everything up neatly; that can safely be left to the pantomime or the farce whose purpose is nothing more than to provide an evening of healthy fun and escapist entertainment. But great drama is different; it causes the audience to leave the theatre at the end of the evening better able to articulate the big questions and with a deeper awareness of the mysteries and complexities of life. When King Lear speaks the line, 'Who is it that can tell me who I am?' we know that Shakespeare is putting into the mouth of his character one of the most profound questions of human existence. The events of the play, the tragic death of the old man, and the ingratitude of his daughters, all leave us pondering the question of our own true identity long after the curtain has come down.

We have witnessed enough already to recognise that the writer of Jonah is an author of considerable skill. As

the action has unfolded before us, we have been person-
ally addressed by a generous God as he deals with a
reluctant prophet and a repentant city. The divine challenge to Jonah has been no less a challenge to us. And
now, as we reach the closing moments of this drama,
there is no escape. The action culminates, not in a satisfying denouement in which all the ends are neatly tied
up, but in a series of questions so provocative and pertinent that it is as if, while the spotlight remains on Jonah,
the houselights have also gone up so that we, too,
become participants in the proceedings, facing the
searching questions of God to which the prophet can
give no satisfactory answers.

What makes us angry?

But Jonah was greatly displeased and became angry.
He prayed to the LORD, "O LORD, is this not what I said
when I was still at home? That is why I was so quick to
flee to Tarshish. I knew that you are a gracious and
compassionate God, slow to anger and abounding in
love, a God who relents from sending calamity. Now,
O LORD, take away my life, for it is better for me to die
than to live."   (Jon. 4:1–4)

From his dishevelled appearance and the smell of alco-
hol on his breath, it was obvious that the man who
turned up in the middle of our fellowship meal was the
worse for wear. He was also hungry and it was a simple
matter to share our food with him. He cleared his plate
speedily and needed no persuading when second help-
ings were offered. No doubt emboldened by the hospi-
tality he had already received, he informed us that he

was homeless and needed a bed for the night. That, too, was easily solved. With the assistance of a willing colleague, I helped him into the back seat of the car and drove the mile or so to the nearby hostel.

I was just beginning to tell myself that I'd done an excellent job of helping a weaker brother and of overcoming my feeling of irritation at having my evening interrupted, when it all went wrong. As we pulled up beside the hostel, our passenger suddenly said in a strangely muffled voice, 'I think I'm going to be sick.' These words proved to be prophetic and they were immediately followed by the contents of his stomach being deposited all over my head. I know there are moments when a warm glow is a pleasant thing, but this was definitely not one of them. His next utterance was one of abject apology. I only just made out the words because the aforementioned emission was running down through my hair and into my ears. I did, however, hear myself shout very loudly, 'O shut up! Just sit still and shut up!' (I think I may have given voice to some stronger language, but, even if I could remember it more precisely, it is unlikely that it would ever be printed in a book for a predominantly Christian audience!) I was furious and the anger that erupted from me was every bit as real, and even more unpleasant, than the substance that had spilled out of my passenger.

Readers of a charitable disposition will probably sympathise with my outburst. But later on that evening – after a shower and a change of clothes to ensure that nothing unpleasant was sticking to my person – there was something stuck in my *mind* that I couldn't get rid of so easily. It wasn't so much the fact that my close encounter with my passenger's dinner had made me so angry, though I regretted my lack of self-control. What really disturbed me was that millions of people in our world had gone hungry that day, thousands of children in developing countries had died of preventable diseases, hundreds of young people had walked homeless on the streets of Britain's cities, and who knows how many people had been denied the opportunity to hear the good news of the gospel and to see it in action because Christians didn't care enough – all that and more, and it hadn't troubled me enough to make me even mildly annoyed.

Jonah's sin – like mine that night – is that he's angry about all the wrong things. It is his irritation, every bit as much as his disobedience, that reveals just how far his heart still is from the heart of God. In the middle of the storm at sea, he could recite his creed and affirm his belief in 'the God of heaven, who made the sea and the land'; in the darkness of the fish's belly he could sing his great psalm of praise, culminating in the cry, 'Salvation comes from the LORD'; but the fact that he cared nothing for the welfare of the Ninevites makes all his religious protestations worthless. He should have been inconsolable at the possibility of their destruction; instead he is furious at the prospect of their deliverance.

In April 1963 Martin Luther King carried his non-violent campaign against racial segregation to the city of Birmingham, Alabama. Finding himself in jail on Good Friday for violating an injunction prohibiting demonstrations, he wrote a letter to the city's white clergy whose support had been at best lukewarm. It would be unfair to categorise them as being as hard-hearted as Jonah, but their failure to empathise with the sufferings of their African-American brothers and sisters is an irrefutable fact of history. Their cautious counsel of prudence and patience was met by King's white-hot righteous anger at the terrible injustice being inflicted on his people. It is the very opposite of Jonah's selfish rage and

it stands as a rebuke to us all who can look on oppression with equanimity or even complete indifference.
May God grant us this kind of anger in the face of every
manifestation of inhumanity and injustice towards others, whatever their race, colour, class or creed

> I guess it is easy for those who have never felt the sting-
> ing darts of segregation to say, "Wait." But when you
> have seen vicious mobs lynch your mothers and fathers
> at will and drown your sisters and brothers at whim;
> when you have seen hate-filled policemen curse, kick,
> brutalize and even kill your black brothers and sisters
> with impunity; when you see the vast majority of your
> twenty million Negro brothers smothering in an airtight
> cage of poverty in the midst of an affluent society; when
> you suddenly find your tongue twisted and your speech
> stammering as you seek to explain to your six-year-old
> daughter why she can't go to the public amusement
> park that has just been advertised on television, and see
> tears welling up in her eyes when she is told that
> Funtown is closed to coloured children, and see the
> depressing clouds of inferiority begin to form in her lit-
> tle mental sky, and see her begin to distort her little per-
> sonality by unconsciously developing a bitterness
> toward white people; when you have to concoct an
> answer for a five-year-old son asking in agonizing
> pathos: "Daddy, why do white people treat coloured
> people so mean?"; when you take a cross-country drive
> and find it necessary to sleep night after night in the
> uncomfortable corners of your automobile because no
> motel will accept you; when you are humiliated day in
> and day out by nagging signs reading "white" and "col-
> ored"; when your first name becomes "nigger," your
> middle name becomes "boy" (however old you are) and
> your last name becomes "John," and your wife and

mother are never given the respected title "Mrs."; when you are harried by day and haunted by night by the fact that you are a Negro, living constantly at tip-toe stance never quite knowing what to expect next, and plagued with inner fears and outer resentments; when you are forever fighting a degenerating sense of "nobodiness"; then you will understand why we find it difficult to wait. There comes a time when the cup of endurance runs over, and men are no longer willing to be plunged into an abyss of despair. I hope, sirs, you can understand our legitimate and unavoidable impatience.[32]

What makes us happy?

> Jonah went out and sat down at a place east of the city. There he made himself a shelter, sat in its shade and waited to see what would happen to the city. Then the LORD God provided a vine and made it grow up over Jonah to give shade for his head to ease his discomfort, and Jonah was very happy about the vine. But at dawn the next day God provided a worm, which chewed the vine so that it withered. When the sun rose, God provided a scorching east wind, and the sun blazed on Jonah's head so that he grew faint. He wanted to die, and said, "It would be better for me to die than to live." (Jon. 4:5–8)

What we now witness is a scene as absurd and surreal as anything in one of Samuel Beckett's plays. While the king and the citizens of Nineveh remain in their fasting and repentance, Jonah, having entered the city from the west, leaves through its eastern borders and settles himself down to see what will happen. He already knows that

God will not destroy the city, and we can only surmise that he is so nonplussed that he cannot even begin to imagine what the future will bring. There is something eerie and unsettling about the scene which is quite unparalleled in any other biblical story. What are we to make of this man who, having delivered God's message and complained about God's grace, can sit dispassionate and detached, seemingly uncaring about the fate of an entire city?

Yet again, tragedy and comedy are intertwined. Jonah, who would willingly have watched Nineveh and its inhabitants burn in the destroying fire of divine wrath, constructs a makeshift booth of leaves and branches to shelter himself from the heat of the desert sun. And, with a delightful touch of irony, the writer immediately adds that God – who has just shown his grace towards the repentant citizens of Nineveh by averting his judgement – demonstrates that same grace to his reluctant and despondent servant by causing a vine to grow up and provide added protection for Jonah. And, for the first and only time in this entire drama, the man who could take no pleasure in the salvation of 120,000 people is in cheerful high spirits! God clearly chooses to use some very odd people in his service.

As we have already learned, however, God's purpose is much greater than the self-centred happiness of his people, and the prophet is about to be taught another lesson. His joy following a good night's sleep under the shelter of the booth he had built and the vine God had provided is short-lived. For in the morning God provides a worm which chews the vine, causing it to wither, and then sends a scorching east wind so that the sun blazes mercilessly on the prophet's unprotected head. Poor old Jonah is plunged back into the depths of depression and once again decides that death would be preferable to his present lot in life.

There is a powerful parable here that we will do well to heed. Jonah's shelter, which is the result of his own efforts *and* God's gracious action on his behalf, is designed to give him protection. But, by its very nature, it can only be temporary. The hungry worm serves only to speed up the inevitable processes of nature by which such a structure would eventually decay. And yet Jonah's happiness is far more bound up with this than with God's redemptive work on behalf of Nineveh. The more you think about it, the clearer the lesson of the parable becomes. Our church traditions, our denominational structures, our style of worship, even our doctrinal statements, are all useful and afford us places of safety and protection. In all of them we can see both the hand of God and the work of humankind, and much of the pleasure we experience in Christian service derives from our sense of being at home in them. But we had better know that they are not identical with the gospel, that they were never intended to last for ever, and that they are less important to God than his rescue plan for the human race and his redemptive purpose for his entire creation. To put it another way; God cares about our churches, but he cares even more about a lost world.

The implications of these truths are enormous. Take, for example, our doctrinal statements. They are important and useful in guiding our thinking on matters of theology, conduct and mission. But they are important in the same way that the map of the London Underground is important. It is the work of very clever people who have designed it to help us visualise the underground system and to get on to the right train in order to travel as quickly as possible from A to B. And there are two things we need to keep in mind. Firstly, we are foolish if we imagine that the 'real' underground is identical with the map. It is, of course, much more complicated than

the diagrammatic representation which has been deliberately simplified. If it attempted to show us every twist
and turning it would be much too difficult to follow. And
secondly, the most important thing is to get on the train
and get to where you are going. When it helps us to do
that, the map has served its purpose. A person who
could recite every detail of every station and every line
on the map but who never got on a train would have
missed the point entirely. And if two people stood on the
platform, arguing so furiously because the name of a station was misspelt on the map that they missed the train,
they would be guilty of getting themselves worked up
about trivialities.

Dare we say that some of our doctrinal disputes have
been of that order? We have been more concerned about
the minutiae of doctrinal map-reading than about assist-
ing our non-Christian neighbours to board the gospel
train. While countless people have lived and died without an encounter with Jesus Christ, we have quarrelled
with our fellow-Christians over secondary details which
make little, if any, difference to Christian faith and practice, or to effective service and evangelism. We need a
proper humility in these matters and we need to be
aware of the fact that the best theological map we can
provide for earnest seekers will always be so much less
than the truth itself

What do we really care about?

> But God said to Jonah, "Do you have a right to be
> angry about the vine?"
> "I do," he said. "I am angry enough to die."

> **But the LORD said, "You have been concerned about this vine, though you did not tend it or make it grow. It sprang up overnight and died overnight. But Nineveh has more than a hundred and twenty thousand people who cannot tell their right hand from their left, and many cattle as well. Should I not be concerned about that great city?"**
>
> **(Jon. 4:9–11)**

The disparity between the prophet's miserable self-centredness and God's infinite compassion could not be wider. Jonah's tantrum over the withered vine is the ultimate disclosure of his poverty of spirit and of the utter repulsiveness of religion without grace. That God's final words are cast in the form of a question simply serves to highlight the wonder of his unfailing love and patience. Not only does that question, contrasting his love for an entire people with Jonah's concern for a plant, allow for only one reasonable answer – of course, God should be compassionate to the city of Nineveh. It also leaves Jonah, despite the fact that it is far more than he deserves, with the final decision and with the last word.

How often do people ask, 'Why doesn't God do something?' The question is always a demand for justice for wrongs done and punishment for the perpetrators of those wrongs. Life would, indeed, be much simpler if God were like that, if every wrong were put right and every evil-doer put behind bars. But those who ask the question forget the truth that Shakespeare puts into the mouth of his great heroine, Portia

> Though justice be thy plea, consider this,
> That in the course of justice, none of us
> Should see salvation: we do pray for mercy,

And that same prayer, doth teach us all to render
The deeds of mercy . . .[33]

In the heart of God, deeper than his justice, deeper than his righteous anger, deeper than his omnipotence, deeper than any logic or rationality, lies an unfathomable and immeasurable compassion for his entire creation and every one of his creatures. It is beautifully expressed in the closing sentences of our story when God asks should he not be concerned for a city which has 'more than a hundred and twenty thousand people who cannot tell their right hand from their left, and many cattle as well.' We detect an echo of the words of Jesus from the cross when he pleads for the forgiveness of his persecutors because 'they do not know what they are doing' (Lk. 23:34) and we sense that we are touching the very heart of God at this point.

The recurring tragedy of the church throughout the ages has been that we are not always willing to let God be God, infinitely loving, unfailingly patient, extravagantly generous, and constantly forgiving. Like Jonah, we are glad to be one of his people, willing to do his work, able to recite our creeds, happy to sing his praises, but too often reluctant to allow him to minister outside of the boundaries of our limited understanding and our inherited traditions. It is time to set God free and to demonstrate his character in our individual lives and in the corporate life of the church. Unarguably, there are times when we must speak against the prevailing philosophies of our day, times when we must defend our right to freedom of religious expression, times when we must be willing to be unpopular and uncompromising in our stand for truth and righteousness. *But none of those is our primary responsibility.*

Of course, we must argue our case as intelligently as we can, we must plan and implement our strategies for mission to the best of our ability, we must use every skill and talent at our disposal to further the cause of Christ and his Kingdom. But above and beyond all those things, we must demonstrate a love that is qualitatively and quantitatively greater than anything else that other systems of belief have to offer. We must fulfil our primary calling to extravagantly dispense God's grace unconditionally and unceasingly to all kinds and conditions of people. And that will impact everything we do.

It will change the way in which we build local church. Good order and tidy membership roles will be less important than offering unconditional inclusion and the opportunity to begin following Jesus from any starting point. Steve Chalke has cut right to the heart of the matter

> Put simply, our task is to be the indisputable proof that God is love. We want to build churches that are inclusive and welcoming to all. Churches where you are in until you jump out, rather than out until you jump in. That means that . . . churches will be messy . . . Why? Because messiness is a consequence of inclusion. Indeed, whenever a local church chooses to be outward-looking and welcoming of all, it will automatically become messier than it was before – it's inevitable. If we take Jesus as our model and invest ourselves in the lives of others as he did, our churches will never be neat, tidy or orderly again. The very act of inclusion necessarily dictates that our churches will be comprised of a diverse collection of people at different points on the journey of faith. They will not believe the same things. They will not have the same values. They will not behave consistently.[34]

It will mean that we will need to ask hard questions about our relationships with people of other faiths. Traditionally, as evangelical Christians, we have seen our mission as winning as many converts as possible to Christianity from other religions. But perhaps we need a new paradigm in our thinking on our mission with regard to other religions. Of course, we will not for one moment weaken in our conviction that Jesus Christ is the unique Son of God, the perfect revelation of his Father's heart, and the only and all-sufficient Saviour for humanity. But we will give greater place to courteous dialogue, in which we listen us much as speak, than to a dogmatic presentation of doctrinal propositions; and perhaps we will even feel able to take the enormous risk of giving less emphasis to proselytising than to producing disciples of Jesus who demonstrate their allegiance to him within the context of the faith and culture in which they have grown up. Brian McLaren speaks tantalisingly of this new way of sharing the good news

> We share the good news of Jesus, seeking to make disciples of all peoples – always inviting, never coercing . . . I must add, though, that I don't believe making disciples must equal making adherents of the Christian religion. It may be advisable in many (not all!) circumstances to help people become followers of Jesus *and* remain within their Buddhist, Hindu, or Jewish contexts. This will be hard, you say, and I agree. But frankly, it's not at all easy to be a follower of Jesus in many "Christian" contexts, either . . . I am more and more convinced that Jesus didn't come merely to start another religion to compete in the marketplace of other religions. If anything, I believe he came to end standard competitive religion (which Paul called 'the law') by fulfilling it; I believe he came to open up something beyond religion – a new possibility, a realm, a domain, a territory of the spirit that welcomes everyone (now including members of the Christian religion) to think again and become like

little children. It is not, like too many religions, a place of
fear and exclusion but a place beyond fear and exclusion. It is a place where everyone can find a home in the
embrace of God.[35]

It will mean a re-examination of our attitudes to those
whose life-styles, particularly in the area of sexual
morality, fall short of accepted Christian standards. If we
are to be the inclusive kind of church for which Steve
Chalke pleads, how are we to react to gay and lesbian
couples, or cohabiting heterosexual couples who seek
fellowship with us? Accepting people does not, of
course, mean endorsing their way of life; but nor should
it mean keeping them at arm's length until they have
come up to the standard we ask. The church, we must
always remember, is full of very imperfect followers of
Jesus. For all of my lifetime, churches have been able to
accommodate people whose unwillingness to tithe and
give generously has indicated their greed, people whose
more than ample girth has revealed their tendency to
gluttony, and people whose wagging tongues have
announced that they have fallen prey to the sin of gossip. Why then should it be any different for those who
are gay or whose sins are just a little more public than
my private failings?

Jesus' invitation to come and follow was made to
twelve very imperfect men who failed him and ran away
at his hour of greatest need. We must allow God to be
God as we make that same invitation today to equally
imperfect people, irrespective of their social standing,
their racial or ethnic origins, their sexual orientation,
their past failures, or their present moral and spiritual
shortcomings. Jesus himself said that his purpose in coming to earth was not to call the righteous but to be the
friend of all kinds of sinners. In living out that purpose,

he demonstrated his Father's heart, spending his days and giving his life for the sake of others without distinction. If we are genuinely to live for others it will mean nothing less than his life lived over again in each of us and in all of our churches, nothing less than allowing God to be God in us. It will probably mean that just about everything we have held dear will change radically and for ever. It will certainly cost us everything, but it will be the best bargain we ever made.

Endnotes

[1] Sally Magnusson, *The Flying Scotsman* (London: Quartet Books, 1981).

[2] John Drane, *Cultural Change and Biblical Faith* (Milton Keynes: Paternoster Press, 2000).

[3] Foreword in Desmond Doig, *Mother Theresa: Her People and Her Work* (Glasgow: Collins Fount Paperbacks, 1976).

[4] *Epistle to Diognetus*, 5 and 6.

[5] Andy Hawthorne, *Mad for Jesus* (London: Hodder & Stoughton, 2000).

[6] David Watson, *Discipleship* (London: Hodder & Stoughton, 1983).

[7] Neil Postman, *Amusing Ourselves to Death* (London: Penguin Books, 1986).

[8] John A.T. Robinson, *On Being the Church in the World* (London and Oxford: Mowbrays, 1977).

[9] Jean Paul Sartre, *Being and Nothingness*.

[10] *Bono on Bono: Conversations with Michka Assayas* (London: Hodder & Stoughton, 2006).

[11] Philip Yancey, *Soul Survivor: How My Faith Survived the Church* (London: Hodder & Stoughton, 2003).

[12] Wallace Boulton, ed., *The Impact of Toronto* (London: Monarch Publications, 1995).

13 Jim Wallis, *God's Politics* (Oxford: Lion Hudson, 2006).
14 Douglas Coupland, *Life after God* (London: Simon & Schuster, 1994).
15 Tony Campolo, *We Have Met the Enemy and They are Partly Right* (Waco: Word Publishing, 1986).
16 Clarence Hall, *Samuel Logan Brengle: Portrait of a Prophet* (New York, The Salvation Army Inc., 1933).
17 Eddie Gibbs and Ian Coffey, *Church Next* (Leicester: Inter-Varsity Press, 2001).
18 Published in *The Times*, 30th January, 2007.
19 Samuel Taylor Coleridge, *The Rime of the Ancient Mariner*.
20 Humphrey Carpenter, *Dennis Potter* (London, Faber & Faber, 1998).
21 Poems and *Prose of Gerard Manley Hopkins*, Selected and Edited by W.H. Gardner (London: Penguin, 1953).
22 William Wordsworth, *The Poetical Works of Wordsworth* (Oxford: Oxford University Press, 1964).
23 Article by David Satterthwaite, Senior Fellow at the International Institute for Environment and Development in *The Guardian*, Wednesday January 17, 2007.
24 Ibid.
25 Ibid.
26 Gary Bishop, *Darkest England and the Way Back In* (Matador, 2007).
27 Ibid.
28 Jacques Monod, *Chance and Necessity* (Alfred A. Knopf, 1971).
29 Ibid.
30 Aldous Huxley, Ends and Means, quoted in Francis A. Schaeffer, *Back to Freedom and Dignity* (London: Hodder & Stoughton 1973.
31 *The Complete Poems and Songs of Robert Burns* (New Lanark: Geddes & Grosset, 2005).
32 Letter from a Birmingham Jail, Martin Luther King.
33 William Shakespeare, *The Merchant of Venice*.

[34] Article in *Christianity* (reprinted in *Salvationist* February 2007).

[35] Brian D McLaren, *A Generous Orthodoxy* (Grand Rapids: Zondervan, 2006).